Curators-Collections

Management of the Arts

Cv/Visual Arts Research Archive

CURATORS-COLLECTIONS
Management of the Arts

978-1-908419-23-1 (Hardback)
978-1-908419-24-8 (Paperback)

Cv/VAR Series ISSN 1476-9980

First edition: December 2011

Curator interviews were first published in
Cv Journal of the Arts Volumes 1-5 1988-92
Then as an anthology:
Curators & Collections
(Editions 1993/1996/2001/2004)

British Library Cataloguing in Publication Data.
A catalogue record of this book is available from the British Library

This edition was printed and bound by
Blissett: Design.Print.Media
www.blissettdigital.co.uk

Cv/VAR Interviews
Transcripts of recordings have been checked, amended
and approved by the featured subjects prior to publication.

Cv Publications
The Barley Mow Centre,
10, Barley Mow Passage,
London W4 4PH, UK
www.tracksdirectory.ision.co.uk

Cv/Visual Arts Research

The survey began in April 1988 as interviews with artists, jewellers, fashion designers and furniture restorers, based at Old Loom House Studios, Whitechapel, launching a quarterly review *Cv Journal of Art and Crafts*. Cv Journal was published to 1992 and the collection of interviews, features and reviews provided the foundation of the Cv/Visual Arts Research archive and subsequent publications.

Cv/*VAR* addresses the fields of academic research, galleries and museums worldwide, and a growing general readership. In this respect the archive has been organised as *Interviews-Artists*; *Curators and Collections*; *Crafts Directory*; *Small Histories*; *Social Studies* and *Studio Work*. Titles are published as books, monographs, as well as CDs and DVDs in Cv's software catalogue.

.

Foreword with acknowledgements

The first edition of Curators and Collections, published in 1997 was based on interviews and features published in the quarterly review: Cv Journal of Art and Crafts (1988-91).

These recorded the launch of the Irish Museum of Modern Art in 1991, the construction of Tate Modern in 1997, as well as exploring special collections at The National Gallery, Courtauld Gallery, The British Museum and Royal Photographic Society. The book contained a comprehensive guide to public and private collections in England, Scotland and Wales, which is revised and updated in this volume. The landscape of the arts has radically transformed in the intervening years, with a tremendous growth in audiences for contemporary art. The study recognises the important role of private foundations and the activity of curators and gallerists in their independent initiatives.

Acknowledgements with great appreciation are offered for their time and generous contribution to the study: Ian A.C. Dejardin, director, Dulwich Picture Gallery; Dr Stephen Deuchar, director, The Art Fund; Jill Constantine, senior curator of The Arts Council Collection; Vincent Honoré, curator, David Roberts Art Foundation; Clare Lilley, curator and head of programme, Yorkshire Sculpture Park. Lucy Byatt, Head of National Programme at The Contemporary Art Society. Dr Christopher Brown, director of The Ashmolean Museum, Oxford. Jock McFadyen and Susie Honeyman of the Grey Gallery; curator James Putnam, gallerist Poppy Sebire, and the writer Edward Lucie-Smith. My personal thanks go to my wife Sarah for her patient and unstinting support, in over two decades gathering the material which appears in this volume.

Nicholas James,
Editor, Cv.VAR
Archive & Editions

Contents

Portrait of an Aristocrat North Bohemian Glass c.1815-20 h.13 cm Courtesy du Verre Paris

Portrait of an Aristocrat
North Bohemian Glass circa 1815-20 H.13cms
Courtesy of Centre Du Verre, Musée des Arts Décoratifs

Centre Du Verre

*Interview with Jean Luc-Olivié, curator,
Centre du Verre, Musée des Arts Décoratifs,
Paris, recorded 8.12.1989*

Cv/VAR. When was the Centre du Verre founded?

JLO. In 1982, by the Musee des Arts Decoratifs with the help of the Ministry of Culture. It is based on a rich collection of old and modern glass for which we had a documentation base, that also served as a study centre. We also have similar reference centres for wallpaper, textiles and toys, and we hope to establish more such bases in other areas in the near future.

Is the Musée des Arts part of The Louvre?

It is included in the Palace of The Louvre, but it is independent from the Museum of The Louvre. It is a private association and is as different as, say the British Museum from The Victoria and Albert Museum. The Musée des Arts Decoratifs was created in the 19th century by a private association of people with the help of the government, but with a certain independence.

What is the earliest period of glass in the collection?

We have some antique pieces, but not an extensive archaeological collection. We have late medieval pieces, stained glass windows of course; a very good series of Islamic and late Renaissance glass. The collection begins to reach international level with this period, but we really have a strong area in the late 18th to 19th century glass, and I think it's possible to say we have the best Art Nouveau glass collection in the world. This collection was created with the artists, including Rousseau, Emile Galle, Lalique, Brocard. The work is mostly French, but we also have one of the major collections of Tiffany Glass in Europe.

So did the artists leave you their work?

Some, and in addition to these acquisitions and gifts we also have purchases and legacies from private collectors. Since 1982 the policy of collecting has become more internationally biased.

Looking at the exhibition of Bohemian Glass in the Centre du Verre.

This present exhibition presents a collection of Bohemian Glass, from the 14th century to contemporary designs?

Yes, this has been organised as a special exchange programme between France and Czechoslovakia; more precisely, between the Museums of Decorative Arts in Prague and in Paris. The next part of the exchange will be an exhibition of French Glass in Prague in 1991. In this exhibition we start with medieval fluted glass found by archeologists in the city of Prague. This piece is from the time of Charles IV, an important Bohemian King and Head of the Romano-Germanic Empire in the late 14th century.

This beautiful Balustre glass dates from the 17th century, and has a strong element of colour infused in its centre.

There are bands of gold and ruby elements set in the glass. This is a very special piece, in terms of the alchemy of glass-making. It is very difficult to achieve technically and gives an extraordinary effect. The 17th

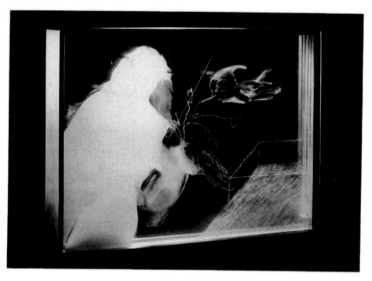

Dana Zámeenikova **How to Catch a Bird** 1981
Ten glass sheets, transparent etched and engraved motifs, mounted in metal
frame, 27 x 28cms Courtesy of Centre Du Verre, Musée des Arts Décoratifs

century Balustre form was an original invention of the Bohemian studios. The Bohemians absorbed the Venetian Techniques and developed their own special skills in engraving glass, as well as some very good qualities of composition.

Here is a later piece a 19th century medallion.
It's a portrait of Prince Alfred von Windischgratz, from the aristocracy of the Austrro-Hungarian Empire, and was engraved by Dominic Biemman, who was the first real modern artist in engraved glass. He was a marvellous engraver as well as being a master draughtsman and painter.

What period is this vase?
At the end of the 19th century, or the turn of the 20th century. It is classic Art Nouveau from the famous manufacture of Loetz. This piece was made by Klastersky Mlyn, and the iridescent surface is influenced in its colouring by Tiffany Glass.

How was it made?
By a kind of oxidation process in a reduc-tion firing, which causes the metallic effect of the glaze. This kind of glass was exported all over the world.

And this Art Deco piece from the 1920s?
This is a fine example of engraving by Josef Drahonovsky, very close to French Art Deco, and it's interesting to remember the continuing close relationship between Prague and Czechoslovakia, which was very active in the 1920s and '30s. For example, this painted glass from 1925-30 shows the influence of Montparnasse, of Picasso and Cubism. Remember as well that before 1918 Bohemia was part of the Austro-Hungarian Empire, and absorbed the effect of the Vienna Secession Movement. There was a very strong cultural interchange between Prague and Paris, as there was also a long tradition of political complicity going back to the revolutions in Europe of 1848.

I don't see many domestic artefacts represented in this exhibition?

The exhibition does not concentrate so much on utilitarian objects as on unique mastepieces of glass creations. This piece is a prime example of the collaboration between two glass artists Stanislav Libensky and Jaroslava Brychtova, entitled Coup Tete 1957. They have developed a form of sculpture in glass by a lost wax process. Libensky has the background of a painter and teacher in Prague, and Brychtova has worked as a sculptor and designer in a factory. They combined their talents to make a very fruitful relationship. They started working together in 1956 and are still making extremely interesting pieces.

This section presents contemporary works?

Yes, this group is more related to visions of utopian architecture, and is made by Vaclav Cigler.

The designs are very clean, clear and geometric. This piece reminds me of the pyramid construction designed by I.M.Pei in the courtyard of The Louvre.

Indeed, it has a certain connection with that. In these works the artist demonstrates their reference to architecture, and plays with the relation of scale to the human figure. These works present a new way to look at reality, rather like the transformation made by the lens in looking at the particular, or far distant; or it could be a new way to discover the space around.

Centre du Verre, Musée des Arts Décoratifs, 107, rue de Rivoli, 75001, Paris. Telephone 1-42-60-32-14. Open Wednesday to Sunday. Closed Monday/Tuesday. Admission charges vary according to the exhibition.

Courtauld Collection

Interview with John Murdoch,
Director of the Courtauld Gallery, London,
recorded 18.05.1994

Cv/VAR. Could you briefly tell me about
your background, before you were appointed
director of the Courtauld Gallery?
JM. Immediately before I came here I was
assistant director in charge of all collections matters at the Victoria and Albert
Museum. I was one of two assistant directors; the other was the administrative
director. I was the curatorial director. We
worked to Elizabeth Estève-Coll, who
was director of the museum.
The programme at the Courtauld Gallery,
including the present exhibition of Impres-
sionist Painting, was arranged before your
appointment?
No, it was arranged entirely after my ar-
rival, and the publication that has been
put together was done at considerable
speed. But since we had most of the material, and we had a major international
scholar on Impressionism, in John House,
available on the staff, who was willing to
do the work and to include all the most
recent thoughts on the Courtauld Collection, it was feasible.
He has written a fascinating introduction it's
something of a revelation about Samuel
Courtauld, and his strategy of forming the
Impressionist Collection. Are you showing
the entire holding?
Remember from your reading of John
House's essay, there are fundamentally
two groups of pictures that Courtauld
put together. One of them is the private

collection; we own most of that. The
other is what we call the public collection, which is the group of pictures he
bought for The National Gallery, specifically in order to strengthen the National
Collections of that class of painting, while it
was still possible. Now our exhibition is of
the private collection pictures that we
normally have here, plus those that he
bought for the private collection, but which
he gave, either to members of his family, or
to close friends.
He gave, or bequeathed certain pictures
to them, and therefore they have not
come to us. So, in order for us to look at
the whole of Sam's private collecting, to
see how all the internal relationships
work, we had to borrow some of those
pictures. The only ones we haven't been
able to borrow are those that have either
been slightly lost to sight; for example,
there is the famous Manet called, Les
Paveurs, which was not available for exhibition. Nor could we borrow the beautiful Seurat, *The Canal at Gravelines*, in the
Berggruen Collection; it had already been
promised to another exhibition.
There was also a Cézanne landscape
which I was very sorry not to have, but
we're so strong in Cézanne, it wasn't a
huge pity. But what we have been able to
borrow, and will absolutely transform
the way people see the collection as a
whole, are Sam's other Renoirs. They're
landscapes, and Sam obviously had a
particular affection for Renoir, as a land
or cityscapist; one of the paintings showing the street of a modern city is of the
Place Clichy. One of those Renoirs which
hasn't been seen in public for a long time,

is a picture called *Spring at Chatou*, which is a beautiful, lyrical vision of the French countryside - joyous. This supplements the way early Renoir is normally represented at the Courtauld, with *La Loge, The Lady at the Opera*; a very urban view, recording the manners of the city.

So how do you balance such a complex mixture of paintings when you're doing a presentation; is it an organic process, an intuitive thing?

Well, in a sense. Had we been able to have absolutely everything, that would have shown Sam's collection as it was originally put together. It would have been an exact mirror of his intentions. One of our hopes has been to show how Sam brought it all together in only the six years he was actively buying, between 1923 and 1929. It was a relatively short period. Obviously he was a very wealthy man and it was a unique opportunity. There were paintings coming back on the market at that time, that had originally been bought by the first generation of Impressionist collectors, and were recirculating through the market.

In a way that gave Sam an opportunity to exercise his own judgement, that was both aesthetic, in terms of what pleased him, in the rooms in which he was going to arrange them, but also reflected his understanding of Impressionism, and its importance for the history of Western art.

It was interesting to read of the resistance to Impressionism, and the committee battles to get the pictures accommodated.

Remember that's about the public collection, and it's really important to get the difference. Yes it's perfectly true, to a certain extent, that Impressionism was controversial, and John House makes all that story very clear. Sam wanted to insert into the National Collection of great pictures, evidence of the great art which had continued to be produced at the end of the 19th century in France, and which would gave an indication of a way forward for art into the present and future. The other thing to remember is the policy background against which The National Gallery operated in the early 1920s, as it is to a certain extent now.

The National Gallery doesn't collect work by living artists, and the Tate does. But the Impressionist pictures bought for the nation were already, as it were, old masters. Sam was a Trustee of The National Gallery, and, despite a few dissident voices, by the 1920s, there was a solid consensus in English art circles that Impressionism - or the work of that group of painters who were known as Impressionists - was important. The controversy, such as it was, had moved on, particularly to Cézanne, and Post-Impressionism was the battlefield of the 1920s. So Sam's purchases of Cézanne and Seurat were really his own. The other thing to remember in the public and private collections; think of what he bought by Van Gogh for the nation, five fantastic, famous masterpieces: *The Chair, the Landscape with Cypresses, Sunflowers,* the close up of Irises, and a landscape. Sam also bought *The Bathers at Asnières* by Seurat for The National Gallery, when critical reaction to the artist in France was pretty much zero. It was only because people like the critic Felix Feneon, by simply collecting these things and holding onto them, as he did with the Bathers, who had saved them for posterity. It was an extraordinary act of courage, and advancing money where one's convictions lay, for Sam to buy such a monumental work in every sense.

Who advised him on his purchases?

Mainly Percy Moore Turner, who set up his independent gallery in 1921-22, just before Sam starts buying. Percy Moore Turner had been a dealer in Paris, so he was in a good position to know what the temperature of the market was. Prices were high then for Impressionists; it was very much a millionaire market, and had been so from the early years of the 20th century. Sam was buying at the top of the market; he wasn't fiddling around to economise. He wanted to buy great pictures and had the money to do it.

He knew that the art market was not like buying and selling rayon, which was his product; where you do close calculations of production costs, overheads and profit levels. As a manufacturer and business-man he knew there was a great differ-ence between the art market and the international manufacturing market, but, as a businessman, he was certainly will-ing to bargain. He respected money, hated its waste, and probably hated more the use of money for stupid luxuries. Sam was a man with a mission. What he was trying to do was make a decisive change in public taste and availability of art in general. He always intended the pri-vate collection to become public in some way.

It eventually did become public through the Courtauld Institute being available to students, and the British public through the Courtauld Galleries being open to general visitors. He intended to give to his gen-eration the opportunity to look at this kind of great art, because it hadn't been available before in this country. He was able to buy it, and do something for civi-lization by making it available.

He was not, however, obsessive. His personal taste I think was much wider than just the Impressionists. He wrote poems about the pictures he loved Rembrandts and Titians, but by buying, what he was doing was changing some-thing in the taste of his generation - broad-ening it, inserting into consciousness Im-pressionism and Post-Impressionism as part of the modern flowering of the Old Master tradition.

The Courtauld Gallery is at Somerset House, Strand, London WC2R 0RN.
Telephone 020 7848 2526

Adults £6 Concessions £4.50 (includes over 60s, part-time and international students) Admission charge includes entrance to all temporary exhibitions and displays.

Free admission for under 18s, full-time UK students, staff of UK universities, registered unwaged and Friends of The Courtauld. Disabled Visitors can bring in a helper for free.

Free Mondays until 14.00 Admission is free on Mondays from 10.00 until 14.00 (excluding public holidays)
Daily 10.00 – 18.00 (last admission 17.30)

Courtauld Gallery Lates: until 21.00
Thursday 30 June, 28 July and 15 September 2011
24 Dec: 10.00 – 16.00 25 & 26 Dec: closed

The Courtauld's Drawings and Prints Room can be visited by appointment.

Duccio – The Maèsta

Italian Painting before 1400
At The National Gallery London

Interview with Jill Dunkerton (JD)
by Sarah Batiste (SB), recorded 29.09.1989

SB. The exhibition is open from the end of November 1989, could you tell me what it is based on?

JD. It's a study of quite a small group of early Italian panel paintings, dating from about 1270 to 1370, only a hundred years. We have a large collection of early Italian panel paintings, but we thought we'd concentrate on eight of the most important and interesting works. Now eight doesn't seem very many, but in fact several are fragments from very large altarpieces. So in one case, one of that eight consists of twelve panels, another consists of nine, and so on. So there are more pictures in the exhibition than you might think at first sight. They are part of a series of three exhibitions at The National Gallery.

Last year we did one on Rembrandt, and next year we'll being doing one on Impressionism. The idea is to demonstrate to the public the sort of study that has been going on at The National Gallery for some time a collaboration between curators, that is, art historians; restorers, who are, if you like, practically minded people, and the scientists. We have a large scientific department who take minue samples from paintings and investigate them in various ways. They identify the paint media and the pigments used. We also have a photographic department who take X-rays and infra-red photographs.

Are the paintings generally stored in the museum, or have you got them from various parts of the world?

No, they are all part of our own collection. There's nothing that has been brought in. We could have made an exhibition two or three times the size, based on our own collection, but we wanted to concentrate it down. In fact it's a very unusual exhibition in that we have borrowed absolutely nothing, other than some bits and pieces, such as artists' tools in a preliminary showcase.

How do you feel about the fact that a lot of the pieces have been dispersed, been broken down from larger altarpieces, and moved to all parts of the world?

Well it's terribly sad, but most of it all happened a long time ago; in the 18th and 19th centuries, or even earlier. We have one altarpiece in the exhibition that probably first got cut about in the early 17th century. We have some evidence that this happened when it was first moved. Then the panels were partly remade in the 19th century, so they have been much altered. It is sad when they are split and dispersed into different collections and obviously, in some ways, it would be lovely to bring them all together, or to bring the survivors together again.

But these early Italian panels are very, very fragile indeed, and it would be difficult and expensive, and very questionable, to bring them all back together. Certainly we don't lend our early Italian paintings to other exhibitions.

Seraphim, Cherubim and Angels Adoring Ascr.Jacopo di Cione, (style of Orcagna), active 1365 to 1398. Wood, irregular top, painted area 37 x 37.5cms (S.Pier Maggiore) Courtesy of The National Gallery London. From Cv Journal 2/4 December 1989

Because they would just disintegrate?
Well it's too great a risk. They are very old, six hundred years old, and very fragile.
Presumably it's only in the latter half of the 20th century that conservation techniques have really begun to identify and carefully look at how these pieces were made?
No, not entirely. In the 19th century, for example, given that they had more limited scientific facilities, there were quite a lot of art historians looking at technical matters. In particular Sir Charles Eastlake, who was director of The National Gallery in the mid-19th century. He wrote important and pioneering books on the subject of technique. Also a wonderful lady called Mrs Merrifield, who translated all sorts of obscure Italian treatises, some of which go back to the 14th century. She was also the first person to translate the famous treatise by Cennino Cennini, and that has a considerable influence on 19th century painting; in the arts and crafts movement and on Pre-Raphaelite painting. They still managed to get quite a lot wrong, but at the same time they developed an interest in the subject. I think the link with the arts and crafts movement becomes very obvious with some of the material in this exhibition.
I was thinking in particular about the way some of the pieces had been conserved previously; you've actually had to undo some of the restoration.
Well yes, that is part of our work here. Paintings constantly need restoration. We hope that we are stretching the interval between each restoration, but no doubt at some point in the future somebody will have to redo our own work. Most of the pictures in this exhibition have been cleaned in the last twenty years. One large altarpiece, the San Pier Maggiore altarpiece by Jacopo di Cione which has twelve panels, I am half way through cleaning. It will not be finished for the exhibition so we shall be showing some panels cleaned and some dirty. They hadn't been touched since about 1840,

certainly they've had no major treatment since they've been at The National Gallery.

Have you made any great discoveries in these pieces which you've looked at, related to the manuscript that Cennini wrote in the 14th century.

We've made discoveries which stem from scientific examination, but also by reconstructing a series of panels using the methods which Cennini describes, brilliantly and in incredible detail in his book. We really have followed them very closely indeed. But what I think I've learnt most about is how workshops were organised and what sort of work could be delegated. Six panels are demonstrated in construction. I was working as the master of the workshop if you like. I was the designer, I did the drawing and the painting, but I had somebody who made the panels, three other people helped put the gesso ground on; three people helped with the gilding, and somebody else made the pigments.

I actually ground the pigments myself, but if I'd been a real master I'd have had a little boy do it, an apprentice. As some of the pigments were the same as the originals, and rather dangerous, they contain lead and mercury, I couldn't use someone else to do it. I had to do it myself with very elaborate precautions in our scientific department. If people are stimulated by the exhibition to work in the same way, I would not recommend they work with the same pigments.

How many people would have worked at one time in these workshops?

I think a big commission by a successful artist Duccio working on The Maesta, he produced a colossal thing in just three years, or so the original documents seem to suggest, and the work is painted on both sides. He would definitely have had assistants, both earlier in application of the gesso ground, and for the gilding, assistants to make the colours. But also we have evidence that there were assistants painting the altarpiece with him, and, though we only have three tiny panels from it, among those panels we have been able to identify a distinctly different hand who has painted the architecture in Christ healing the man born blind.

In the enormous altarpiece by Jacopo di Cione, which is single sided but as big as The Maesta, there are also quite a lot of documents associated with it. There we have a sort of specialist designer, a painter called Niccolo di Pietro Gerini, a sort of Mr.Fixit who turns up in all sorts of documents organising all manner of things restoration projects, painting of altarpieces, painting of frescoes, and so on. He seems to have been the instigator of the project, but the main painter was Jacopo di Cione. There are several other people mentioned in the documents, so we've been able to speculate as to what their role may have been.

Could you take me through the reconstruction of a panel?

All the pictures in the exhibition are painted on panels made of poplar. The reason for that is there was a great shortage of timber in the 14th century, and any really good timber, like oak, had to go into ship building and the construction of houses. Poplar's not a very good wood because it's soft and spongy and not very strong, so you have to cut very thick panels. We actually had some trouble in getting poplar for the exhibition, because it has virtually no modern use. According to timber merchants it's used for making matchsticks, and that's about it. However I managed to get some through the London College of furniture, where it's used to make reproductions of keyboard instruments. It is difficult to work with and has several faults, which don't seem to have bothered the early Italian painters at all. In fact you find great knots in the wood which often caused disruption in the paint surface.

They may not have not have minded, or they may have had very little choice. They did take certain precautions to stop the knots breaking through. For example, before putting on the ground they nearly always covered the poplar with linen canvas, as we have in our reconstruction. Once the linen canvas is on you build up the ground, always gesso, which is Italian for gypsum - calcium sulphate. It is built up in two stages first a coarse layer, gesso grosso, then layers of a smoother gesso called gesso sottile. That is quite difficult, because to get the layers to unite properly you have to do it all in one run. Cennino says, If necessary you may have to stay up all night to brush on the layers of gesso. Certainly John England, the head of our framing department, and his two assistants, had a pretty frantic day on six, really rather small panels, getting on all the layers of gesso in one go.

So after the gesso is laid, do you have to rub down the surface?

You then have to smooth it. All these panels have gold leaf on them, and to have a good surface to gild on, the gesso must be smoothed until it's like ivory. Because the point of gilding, as people will see in the reconstruction panels, is that the gilding was supposed to imitate solid gold. You were meant to have the illusion when you went into a church, that you were seeing these paintings against blocks of gold. So the gold leaf, which was applied by water gilding in almost exactly the same way as today's method, was burnished to this really deep liquid gold effect, which is now totally lost on the paintings, which are now cracked and worn through age. Certainly for us doing these reconstructions, that was quite a revelation.

It must have been stunning, especially in a dark church with candles burning.

Exactly. So many of the techniques they used demonstrate the fact that the light sources were very different from the way modern galleries show art now. We show the pieces well-lit so people may examine the details, but they should imagine that in the 14th century they didn't have much clear glass, so not much daylight was getting through, and that candle light moves. So a lot of the decoration was designed to exploit that flicker of the light. Though you have these great solid blocks, you would also stipple and punch the gold so that it sparkles and reflects as the light moves.

Was there a range of specific colours which were always used?

They were very limited in what they could use. Some came from natural mineral sources, of which the most famous is the blue pigment Lapis Lazuli, which came from the mines in Afghanistan, where it is still found today. It was very, very expensive, more than gold, and was brought in on the silk routes. It was used to demonstrate how well-off the patrons were, by having a lot of Lapis in their pictures.

The red pigment vermilion was probably made artificially, though there is a natural source for it as well. The bright yellow pigment and the various lead tin yellow dye stuffs were probably bought from an apothecary, and the painter then processed them to some extent, making them into a paint bound with egg. And the colours in the works, the pigments, are used very pure with no messing around, mixing and toning down.

Tell me something about the patronage of these paintings?

All the pieces in the exhibition were made for ecclesiastical settings. Sometimes, for example- the Maesta for Sienna Cathedral, the work was commissioned by a committee of works, that is, various philanthropists coming together to raise money and organise the project. Sometimes it was paid for by private patronage. Others were paid for by religious orders, like the Franciscans of Santa Croce.

After the paint was laid, were the panels varnished?

That we don't know. Cennino Cennini is a bit difficult over that, he fudges the issue rather. He describes various varnishes and tells you how to do it, but he is not particular as to how often it was done. There's been a general belief that they were not actually varnished, that they liked the eggshell sheen of tempera. However, one of the altarpieces, the San Pier Maggiore altarpiece actually has documentation for the panels to be taken somewhere to be varnished.

When I came to clean one of these panels, we looked at it more closely and discovered around the edges, where the paint must have been covered by the frame, that in fact threr were traces of an orange brown substance, which was found to contain the same ingredients as recipes of the 14th and 15th centuries. It would have produced a clear, very high gloss finish. It may have been exceptional and does not mean we are going to place a glossy varnish all over our early Italian altarpieces.

Do you have a favourite work?

I suppose I have certain favourites. I think the ones I love above all are the Predella panels from the Ugolino Santa Croce altarpiece, *The Betrayal of Christ*, *Christ Carrying the Cross* and *The Deposition*. Ugolino was the most stunning and original of the colourists. He uses a very limited palette and sets colours against one another in an unusual way. They are very, very moving pictures.

Art in the Making Italian Painting before 1400
was exhibited at The National Gallery, London,
from 29th November 1989 to the 28th February 1990.
The exhibition was sponsored by Esso UK plc

Art In The Making 2

Impressionism

Interview with John Leighton, Curator of 19th century painting at The National Gallery, London, recorded 27.11.1990

Cv/VAR. How was this exhibition put together?

JL. The fifteen paintings are all from The National Gallery, the work of seven different artists in the Impressionist movement. It's the third in our series of Art in the Making exhibitions, where we look in detail at the materials and techniques of the artists. The idea to focus on the Impressionists really stemmed from the work that had been carried out by our conservation department on two paintings: *Bathers at La Grenouillere* by Monet, and *Boating on the Seine* by Renoir, both of which produced results in analysis which were quite interesting, and in some ways unexpected.

Were the paintings in need of restoration?

Well both were restored on acquisition. *La Grenouillere* had quite a thick coating of yellow varnish, especially over the right hand side, we think to give a more finished look to the painting, or to tone it down.

Looking at Boating on the Seine by Renoir, 1879-80.

This work was painted with a very limited number of pigments, six plus white. All but one of these were modern 19th century inventions, and the effects we see here the translucency, the brilliance, the luminos-ity, would have been unthinkable without the 19th century innovations in paint-making.

Because the quality of pigment significantly improved?

Yes, a lot of work had been done in developing manufactured pigments. For example, it was only very early in the 19th century that a modern equivalent became available for natural ultramarine, a pigment widely used in the history of art, but extraordinarily expensive, as it was made from semi-precious stones transported from Afghanistan. You can buy it even now, but it costs £84 for ten grams, so you can imagine the effect for painters of this manufactured pigment.

Liberation.

Exactly.

This Renoir is scintillating, the painting seems to have lasted so well.

It has. Another feature of the new pigments was their stability. We know of pigments in the past that have been unstable, fugitive colours, that have disappeared, often transforming the pictures. As far as one can tell, the Impressionists pigments were extremely stable and have survived very well, with the results you can see here.

Looking at The Umbrellas, (Les Parapluies) by Renoir, 1881-86.

This is a two-part painting, developed over a number of years with a marked change in style.

We'd always suspected that this painting was created in two distinct phases. An X-Ray of the picture shows the figure of a woman on the left in an entirely different costume, frilled with a high lace collar. The group on the right has been painted in A soft and feathery style, more akin to Renoir's work in the 1870s, and has a very bright and luminous blue, with cheerful and brilliant colours. On the left, however, you have forms which are more clearly defined, much more structural. You almost feel the dress has been carved and chiselled. Perhaps the most striking is the colour, which is quite severe. When we began to analyse it in depth, using for example paint cross-sections, we discovered, in terms of its layer structure and the materials used, it is perhaps the most complex picture that's ever been examined at The National Gallery. It's clearly a picture that gave Renoir a lot of trouble. He struggled to resolve the conflicts between colour and drawing, between movement and qualities of sculptural form.

Can we pinpoint a reason why he changed his approach, could one suggest Cézanne's influence?

Yes, Cézanne is relevant. But if one dates the first phase of the right side of the painting to the early 1880s, intervening between this and the second phase, around 1885-86, is a trip to Italy, where Renoir is known to have admired the work of the ancients. He talks of introducing classical qualities into his art, of having come to the end of the road in Impressionism, and being troubled that, in his own words, he couldn't draw or paint.

At this time he stayed with Cézanne in the South of France, which does seem to have had some stylistic influence. The painting of the trees here, and the diagonal hatched strokes are really a hallmark of Cézanne.

His later work retrieves the shimmering brilliance of colour. How long did this classical phase last?

Through the 1880s in its most severe form, and well into the '90s. I think Renoir began to feel ill at ease with its hardness, but we can't really explain why he chose to leave the painting in its divided form. Perhaps it's because it is Renoir's last large-scale painting of modern urban life in a contemporary setting. After this he begins to move away into more timeless themes of nudes in landscapes, and subjects drawn from classical mythology.

The Umbrellas is a very charming picture and has Renoir's unique social observation.

Yes, it's very engaging. It's curious that Renoir didn't exhibit it straight away. He eventually sold it to his dealer Durand-Ruel. It wasn't put on public display until early this century, and I wonder whether the disjunctions in style would have been too glaring for a contemporary audience. It has taken some time for the picture to develop the tremendous appeal it now has.

Art in the Making 2: Impressionism was exhibited at The National Gallery, Trafalgar Square, London, from 28th November 1990 to 21st April 1991. The exhibition was sponsored by Esso UK

Celtic Metalwork

From the Trove of Derrynaflan

Featured in The Work of Angels* at the British Museum, London, 28th November 1989 to 29th April 1990.Interview with Dr Michael Ryan, Keeper of Irish Antiquities at the National Museum, Dublin, recorded 28.11.1989

Cv/VAR. Part of this collection was discovered in Ireland, when and where was this?
MR. This hoard was found in the monastery of Derrynaflan, Co.Tipperary, on the 17th February 1980. It was brought to the museum by the finder the following day, and I remember distinctly the shock I felt when it was unpacked. And immediately, I must say, I saw it not only as a great find, but also as a horrendous nightmare, with all the legal complications of state treasure trove, the status of treasure trove in Ireland administratively, what kind of reward to pay, and how to balance the fact that the finder had not got permission of the landowners when he dug up the find, with his exemplary behaviour in reporting it promptly.

Was it a chance discovery?
No, he had been using a metal detector, but it has been unlawful since 1930 to dig without a licence for archeological objects in Ireland. Since 1987 it is also unlawful to dig using a metal detector, or to possess a metal detector on an archaological site. The law is constantly being tightened because we are determined to stop the plundering of archeological sites.

One notes the fantastic quality and condition of the pieces in this exhibition. How did they survive so well, or has there been a lot of restoration?
I should start by saying that one of the pieces in the hoard, the bronze basin which covered it, is very decayed. It was placed as a kind of roof over the other objects in the pit. The chalice was found standing upright in what had amounted to a controlled environment for over a thousand years. The paten is probably the most complex piece in the find. It has over two hundred and fifty components. It was partly dismantled and had to be rebuilt. In fact my colleagues and I spent a lot of time debating with the British Museum about this three dimensional jigsaw and how to rebuild it.

Was the trove hidden from marauders at the time?
It was hidden, but we don't know from whom, or why or when. It must have been a time of stress. The latest object in the find is the chalice, which dates probably from the eralier 9th century AD. It's a little bit worn from use, but not heavily, so it was probably not very long made before it was buried. You could take it that the whole hoard was probably buried in the 10th century.

We're looking at an ancient door handle, where is it from?
It's from a place called Donore, in County Meath. It was found on a river bank in 1984, and was acquired some months later by the National Museum. I excavated the find spot. A group of objects was discovered there which seems to have been the metal components of a great wooden structure

possibly the door of a church, or a very large sarcophagus in which a saint's body had been placed. The door handle itself is composed of a beautifully engraved plate of tinned bronze and a magnificent cast animal head and a frame. The three pieces can be assembled in exact relation to each other, and the maker put little assembly marks on the backs of the pieces. We reproduced the relationship of those marks and restored this wonderful handle with its escutcheon plaque. The handle has a lion's head, as you might find in a Roman temple, translated into the style of the monasteries of Ireland. Indeed the same style of work was used by the great scribe of the Lindisfarne Gospels.

Would the maker have known of Roman Art?
He could have, in theory, been influenced by Roman traditions. Whether directly or transmitted by intermediaries, we don't know. For instance, if he had seen rough sketches by a traveller abroad. We do know that, if we look behind the superficial decoration, and the structure of the objects, we can find a relationship with the Roman world, probably through Christianity. Christianity was, of course, the great spreader of Roman tradition throughout Europe. Also the Roman influence could have come through the Anglo-Saxons, say through the Christian Church of Northumbria, for example. So it tells a very complex story of a number of streams of tradition coming together to produce a new art. It's an art which relies on a simple technology , but the technology is used to tremendous effect.

Tell me about the methods involved, is this piece beaten or inlaid?
The plate is a hammered disc of bronze, which was then tinned and engraved.
But there are two different textures?
The moulding which you can see around the outside is seperately made and cast. The animal head, which is quite independent, was cast in one piece, probably in a clay mould. The eyes of the animal are inlaid with brown glass, which superficially resembles amber. The mould would have originally been made from a wax model.
It's wonderful.
Yes, it's superb. If you look at the detail on it, the intricate ornaments on the piece, and then go into the British Library and look at the Lindisfarne Gospels, you will see exactly the same tradition, of the same period.

This piece is a silver paten from the 8th century AD, found in Derrynaflan. Can you describe its details?
First I should explain that a paten is a dish for the Eucharistic Bread. But this is a very large example at about thirty seven centimetres in diameter. That places it in a very early tradition of Eucharistic Plates. In the Middle Ages the fashion developed of making very small plates which sat on the rims of chalices. This belongs to a much earlier tradition. There is a story in Gregory of Tours History of the Franks, of a Count who wanted to cure his foot of disease by washing his feet in the paten. That would imply something of the size of the basin. Now this paten is an extraordinary structure. It's a very complicated piece

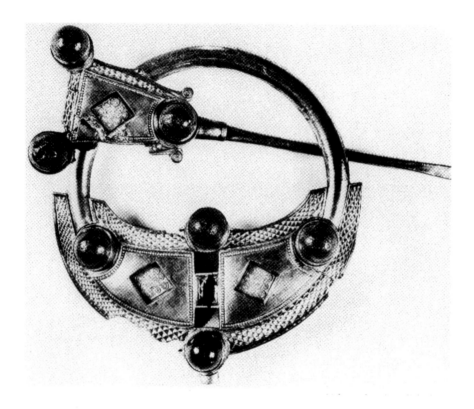

Silver Gilt Brooch with gold filigree and amber settings, from Loughmoe, Co.Tipperary. Irish, 9th Century. Collection: The National Museum of Ireland.
By permission of The British Museum
From Cv Journal 3/1 March 1990

the top part has about two hundred and fifty principal components. There are twelve frames of filigree settings around the upper surface. Each of these carries a central enamel stud, magnificently inlaid. The filigree is made up two to three wires thick, or consists of gold with wires set on edge and soldred into place. If you look carefully you can see very clear motifs there are men, beasts, stags and snakes, then there are the conventional Celtic patterns of spirals and scrolls.

Is there any significance in the designs on the enamel studs?

Yes, you can see the design of the cross. The other ornaments seem partly symbolic also. The little filigree scene of the stag and the snake is obviously a Christian episode. There is an eagle, which is based on an Evangelist symbol, or could sometimes have meant Christ, who was regarded as an eagle in early Christian tradition. Now if you look around the rim you can see knitted or moulded silver and copper wire.

Yes, it's made in a kind of cross-latticed v-shape.

But if you study the whole circumference you see that the maker changed the stitch every few centimetres to give a different texture and pattern, and also perhaps to display virtuosity. On the sides you see twelve beautiful inlaid red, blue and yellow enamel studs. These are held in place by twelve stamped gold foil panels.

What condition did the paten arrive in?

The superstructure was more or less intact, though parts were decayed quite badly. It was covered with a wash of copper salts from the decaying basin and many of its original components were detached. But we were very lucky, because the craftsman who made the paten engraved the surface of the dish with twelve letters in Irish script to match the twelve filigree frames that were set onto it. He also put corresponding construction marks on the undersides of some of the detached components.

Would that indicate he had assistants in his workshop to whom he gave instructions, like a key coding?

It certainly implies something of the kind. It also shows that the person who made the piece may have been literate, as in a monastic workshop rather than a secular one. The letter K is included, which doesn't occur in the Irish alphabet. It is common to the Latin and Greek alphabet.

This period of history is known as the Dark Ages, because of the Viking invasions etc. Do you think they might have concealed the treasure during such an invasion?

Well this period is only known as the Dark Ages in Britain. Everywhere else it's called the Early Medieval Period. Anglo-Saxon civilisation in Britain at the time was wonderful and influential. The term Dark Ages was popularised by a BBC programme in the 1950s. If we could only get away from it and start looking at these things for what they are; great products of important cultures and civilisations. Some of them were abortive civilisations, but they achieved remarkable things, both culturally and technologically.

---

*The title of the exhibition is taken from the writings of Gerald of Wales in the late 12th century, which record his response to the artistry of an early medieval gospel book seen at Kildare.

Launch of the Irish Museum of Modern Art

Interview with Declan MacGonagle, director of the Irish Museum of Modern Art, Dublin, by David Rose Recorded in February 1991. First published in Cv Journal 4/2 1991

DR. *Declan MacGonagle, thank you very much for giving me this interview. Can we begin with your relationship with the building, and the new gallery's relationship with the building how you see an old formal building with a heavily loaded history interacting with the concerns and language of 20th century art?*

DMcG. Well I think you have put your finger on it by saying that it is loaded with history. Increasingly it is my understanding that those artists that I would find interesting and, I think, have the most to contribute, are those people who are trying to deal with all sorts of loaded histories in different contexts. Obviously the loaded history here is quite specific to the complex relationships with England, indeed with Europe, for in fact the architecture of the building refers to a European tradition as well.

I have said right from the beginning, even before I was involved in the project, when it was first mooted and there was a debate in Dublin about the advisability of the RHK (Royal Hospital at Kilmainham) building, against the 19th century warehouse solution in the new docklands financial district; that in setting up a museum from scratch in this country at this time, and to deal with the future questions that we shall face, then such a

museum should be located in the context of the neighbourhood where those histories are present and lived through every day. Because that gives us, gives me, an opportunity to make all of that the subject of our work. That would have been much more difficult to do in a state physically disconnected from the community, granted that the other proposal was a 19th century warehouse.

But the idea of converted warehouses is a product, of a sort, of New York the result of the process that took over New York in the '60s, where people moved into warehouses for economic reasons, and out of that came this loft style living, and also the use of these economically viable spaces. So it was never God-given that modern art should be contained in these warehouses. It was simply a set of social, political and economic circumstances that created the pattern. I think we may be starting something from scratch here, with the chance to examine the pattern, decide what is useful within it, and either adopt it or move away from it.

I think the beauty of the decision here, which may have been made for other reasons, is that it is a fantastic opportunity to set about creating something capable of dealing with both the present and the future, and doing it by using the past, and bringing into play in a contemporary arena all those historical references that, one view would have it, should remain outside art. My view is that is the substance of art, and that's what gives art its value in society. It is absolutely fundamental. I can see this as a container that holds the museum, but we're not simply a tenant in a conveniently maintained building. This building, the fabric of this building, its history, the site, which pre-dates the building in relation to the development of Dublin, are going to be part and parcel of the development of our work.

I think we will be coming back to aspects of that, because everything we will talk about does come back to that! Originally, when people were discussing the possible venues for IMMA, there was some confusion as whether there was going to be a museum of modern art within the RHK, as you say, a tenant within the building, or whether the RHK was going to be itself that museum. Now clearly you are taking the second sense, but at the same time, as I understand it, conferences and banquets and so forth, will also continue here. I am wondering if there is a certain amount of conflict there, between something that is bound to be marketed (or will it be marketed?) as a superior venue where people can look good. Would certain functions be deemed inappropriate for example? Would you turn them down? What interface will there be between the people who come here on a conference, and the museum itself?

The starting point is that this whole site will become the museum of modern art. We will refer to it as being at the RHK, because people, taxi drivers, know where that is. Also the reference means that you do conjure up those historical associations and references. The building is a gift on a number of levels the conceptual level, but also the practical level, because it is built round a quadrangle with four wings; with the north wing, in a sense, the most elegant, sort of grandiose. That is where the rooms are that are used for conferences and seminars and banquets, state occasions and so forth. I have walked through them with many artists who have been visiting from outside Ireland to have a look, with the possibility of working in the future. Their reaction has always been that this is a work of art of Ireland. The north wing is already, with the banqueting hall and chapel, a very powerful cultural statement. It contains certain values, it is very clear what it is about. And it is going to be very difficul for artists to engage with that, because it is like engaging with the work of another artist. But the architecture releases us from the problems if we go with it. If we work against it, I think it poses enormous problems.

In the context of this building yourself into the fabric, can I raise the subject of the title Gallery or Museum? Are these really different concepts, or is Museum a buzz word, simply because Oxford and New York have museums of modern art?

I think it was a buzz word, but again I take up this issue of the advantage of the disadvantage. People say to me that it should be Gallery of Contemporary Art, for instance, but I think you can invest language with new meaning. Just as new functions are being created for this old building. The word museum in Europe does not carry the meaning of a dead place. In fact, I see it as one of the tasks of the museum, to redefine the word, explore its meaning and history. Neither I as an administrator, nor the building, are transparent mediators. We are making decisions, we are making things happen. And whatever happens doesn't arrive from outer space, with a sort of authoritative glow of museum status around it. And the name does link it to other museums of modern art, a constituency is identified, and the requirement is fulfilled in identifying the national role - the Irish Museum of Modern Art. And it does give us the opportunity to counterpoint, say, the Museum of Modern Art in New York, which is a particularly dominant, modernist model of what a museum can and should be in the 20th century, while we are late 20th and into the 21st century, and the world is much more confused, fragmented. So from scratch we can question these earlier models, confounding or contradicting some expectations, complementing others. Nothing should be taken as given, everything should be up for reconsideration.

Working with living artists extends the view of what is art. You are clearly not going to be the curator of a collection of masterpieces, and leaving it at that.

We have a number of functions to cover. I do think that we have to demonstrate, right from the start, that we can curate a collection of masterpieces, if that is necessary for the programme, but that we are also capable of generating other readings of those masterpieces, and other readings of what art is, and is for. And we will do that, as you said, by working largely with living artists. So, yes, I don't see myself as a curator of dead objects. I actually think that the art object is simply evidence of the process that has gone on in creating it, and is evidence of the process that can go on when the viewer comes to engage with the work. Now, if we borrow works from another museum, we have to look after them, have lighting controls and so on, but we only really create a critical presence for ourselves, and so be an effective institution, if we operate with a sort of critical momentum. In other words, we will not borrow from another museum just because of the fame of an artist, but because there is a critical point to be made with those borrowings, and so underpin our whole attitude. To be able to draw upon the widest possible evidence, we need to be capable of operating as a Museum with a capital M, as well as something which questions it. There is a double rle we are establishing a museum, but also questioning one.

We have other modern galleries in Dublin the Hugh Lane Municipal Gallery, the RHA Gallagher Gallery, the Douglas Hyde. Do you think the presence of the IMMA somehow destabilises them?

Not at all, I think it actually releases them from a lot of pressure. Again I am a believer in seeing everything as an opportunity. We will be having regular meetings, because I think there is a fantastic opportunity at the moment, which has come about totally fortuitously, that there is a new beginning right across the city (referring to new appointments at other galleries), and there is the regeneration of The National Gallery as well. The sooner we can sit down and say, here is the long term strategy for all artists, examine our critical function in both Ireland and the wider area, the better. We can do that much better together than individually. And I am happy to talk and tell anybody how I am working. The city will get more if we complement, and we should. The history of museums and galleries has been that people in the main don't believe it's for them. That has been a tragic circumstance for artists to work through, a feeling that a gallery cuts you off from a community. What I would like to do here is to establish this institution as one where the work shown is a way of connecting with the community. This is a very privileged building, a very privileged site, and I am sure there is resistance in an area like Kilmainham to the idea of this building even. I would be very curious to find out how many people have been through the gate from this particular neighbourhood.

When people say to me that the museum is very far away from the city centre, my answer is that it is not very far away from Kilmainham. The attitude that describes it as far away implies that art and culture are for people who do not live in Kilmainham. But art, to be of value, must address all sorts of people, and the key to that is diversity of programming; not just in terms of exhibitions, but in terms of the way we mediate those exhibitions. And again, the architecture of this building lends us to that diversity of programming. We can create within the community, rather than imposing a programme. How we sell it to a community is a different thing.

I know that you believe that the very concept of regionalism is something that has been invented at the centre. At last year's conference on Regionalism and the Centre at TCD, I did not hear the notion expressed that possibly,

instead of centre and regions, or margins, or periphery, what you have is a series of centres, each with its own hinterland. I lived in West Cork for many years, and people said that was remote, but, to take your point, I wasn't remote from the nearest village, and Cork people do not think they are remote from Dublin; they think they are central to Cork. In Skibbereen they don't think they are remote, unless they happen to be in Dundalk! So it moves on down to one homestead, or one lonely farm.

Absolutely. If I had stayed in Derry, the task would have been, not to have worked with bigger and bigger international names, but to embed the practice further in the community. The function, the process, is the important thing. Regionalism comes out of the 19th century idea of the nation state which created a centre and regions. That's a hierarchical definition that you value the less, the further way you are from the metropolitan centre.

All of that is breaking up, it's not where the new thinking is coming from. It is coming from people on the edge, socially or geographically. You can set up a model of something working in a specific locality to the highest possible standards. I am not one who believes in the term or philosophy community arts, because it is a sort of in-built sub-standardisation of work the real thing, and then community art. The true practice is one of enabling and empowering people to make their own decisions and not receive a script from elsewhere. Regions tend to be administrative areas, but there is a far more vital and important social demarcation of a society that goes on geographically, and politically, and economically. What I'm suggesting is that we engage with that mapping which is people's minds already, that we go right through into the fabric that people understand and live their lives through. That is what we previously engaged with when we were all part of the common currency. The 19th century created the concept of the artist, who is someone disconnected from society, but that notion, and the one of the avant-garde, of the artist being ahead, is one that, now we are coming to the end of the 20th century, can be returned; we can re-establish the idea of locality and the artist (and therefore art), as a product o the social environment. If we operate on that basis, if you unlock that relationship, it is just extraordinary what can actually happen.

With the Orchard Gallery you deconstructed the idea of the gallery in the Bond Street sense, it couldn't have been further from that. The walls melted and the gallery merged with the city. I know it is called Orchard because it is in Orchard Street, but one does have a rather nice resonance there. But then you had the walls of Derry, it could almost be a construct, or paradigm of engagement with environment. But did you engage with the walls, and do you see scope for that here?

One of the last things we did before I left was an architectural exhibition. We set out to demonstrate that Derry was not a hole in the ground, but was built in the context of a mainstream European tradition. Comparative studies by students from Queen's showed very clearly that Derry, Dublin and European cities all developed organically, whereas a city like Belfast went from being a village, an organic unit, to being a city overnight, linked with the North of England industrial cities which are now facing enormous problems about identity. I can see Dublin as not being that different from Derry therefore, because of its history. And the contemporary reality is very interesting in terms of the way the city is changing, and how that is merged in the city of Dublin, both negatively and positively.

So the principle is no different from me addressing the locality of Derry and doing certain things as a result. What I would suggest here is that we address the principles that underline the development of any communiy. So yes, that process of melting the walls, which is a very good phrase, could take root here as well. I also believe this building allows us almost to say that the walls are already being somewhat melted, because it is porous. This is a phrase I find myself using more and more; a porous museum that allows both a flow in and out, and that is crucial I think, for this particular institution.

When you were at the ICA in London, you must have had a relationship with the neighbourhood. Was it that the culture perhaps defeated you?

No, no. One of the things that I learned in Derry was that I'm only as effective as I would like to be in a situation where a number of constituencies have to be addressed. It would have deepened my feeling of effectiveness there if we had had a neighbourhood which would have presented a challenge to the institution, or if it was attempting to be international and local at the same time. It would have been a very interesting challenge. When I went back to Derry, I carried that understanding with me, which meant that I was able to work so that the local and international were not mutually exclusive at all. Personally I found it hard to feel just whom I was addressing at the ICA. That was a curious experience, having come from a very, very particular place, where there was no doubt who were being addressed.

Set between Buckingham Palace and the Admiralty! Would you like to have been director of the Irish Museum of Modern Art if it had been in the Financial Services Centre?

No, I wouldn't have been interested.

I expected that answer. You had room to manoeuvre and develop the programme at the Orchard largely because you were starting from scratch, and so you are here, but the chain of command I suppose is rather different. You would presumably have a board that knows its own mind (insofar as any board knows its own mind), rather more clearly than the City Fathers in Derry?

Well I should correct you there, because nobody knows or thinks they know their own minds more than the local authority counsellors!

Let's address this thing of the great national institution. There would presumably be pressure on you, perhaps you would even wish, to generate blockbuster exhibitions, lavish catalogues, that sort of thing. Does that conflict at all, because that addresses itself to a constituency which is very used to that sort of art, to what they call the higher art audience perhaps. Would you still hope to involve the commu-

nity in this, or would it have to be like renting out the place for functions, rather discreet?

No, no. I am already negotiating with other institutions for exhibitions or projects that they would be initiating. As I did in the Orchard, where somebody has created an exhibition, is to work with an artist for that to be remade, recreated, rethought even, in many cases, for the new context. That's the way I am working again. We'll start at a modest level curator, and education and community coordinator. The administrative staff is here already, we will add a few people to that and have security people. We have to develop our own identity and we may find in time that we need to provide more in one area than in another.

We have to make sure that the functions that are our tasks are catered for. In time we will be collecting works, we will be collecting projects, so we will need someone who is called the curator to look after this. But hopefully the collection will be unlike any other, and thereupon call on different skills from simply cataloguing dusty objects in a dusty store room. Where someone says, thi object is too precious to go on show, I think you have to question what you are doing having the object. There is a practice which has created in some cases, a situation where the conservation department is only happy if the work is kept in a dark room. There's a balance to be struck.

They need to remember that today is yesterday's future.

Absolutely. We have to be saying, what is this for? And what must underline the institutional momentum all the time is, what is the institution for? And that's a debate, I'm not suggesting a consensus. I hope some of the things we do here will benefit that sort of debate in the context of museum conferences or whatever. We will add to the relationship between forward programming and heritage.

Would you be happy with charges?

We have debated this in the last six months, we have debated everything. We won't be charding for general admission. We will charge for special exhibitions, and we will look at it again in several years time and see what the reality is. But I think we are in a very good position because we have other activities that can generate income. I think we will invite donations, but open and free to the public, yes, and for special exhibitions, children would be free, and all sorts of concessions.

Is disabled access catered for?

That has been catered for, yes. We have lifts to all floors and ramps to the lifts. And we have bought the entire Gene Lambert exhibition of photographs of people with disabilities, and we will show some of those in our opening exhibition. Early next year we are going to do a major exploration of this issue. Not just disabled artists, but the representation of this. That's something we should be quite aware of.

Presumably you will not give up the concerts and recitals?

We would extend those, in fact, and identify other ways in which the music programme and theatre can be extended, and where it can link with the visual arts programme.

With your position as head of a national institution, do you see that you will spend a lot of time being diverted from the primary task by attending international conferences, that sort of thing? How would you see yourself on a spectrum that runs up to say, Sir Roy Strong, or Sir John Pope-Hennessy?

I wouldn't actually. The only link is the designation as director of the museum. I know the sort of thing you are talking about. I think we actually have different agendas, and that it is simply a coincidence that I am called director of museum, and so are they. Our definitions of director, of museum, of art, of culture, would be very different. So I don't see myself even being on that spectrum. I am an artist first, I am not a curator in the sense of having administrative qualifications, or an art history degree. But I feel that is a major advantage.

My experience has shown that the key thing will be developing relationships with living artists. If an artist trusts you and believes in the critical opportunity, things happen. We may buy one work and be given another by the artist. So my training in that sense, and experience, is a great asset. Where we have to bring in scholarship, we will bring it in, the institution will provide for it. But I hope that my sort of, well, off-centre, or off-mainstream academc, curatorial role will assist this museum to become something that is quite separate and different. Separate is the wrong word - something unique, and therefore something of this time.

Declan McGonagle
First director IMMA

From Cv Journal 4/2 July 1991

Finally, in Fortnight, in December 1989, you said in an article, that one of the goals of cultural activity should be to try and pose the question, Who are we and what can we be? That was the article called Out of Hibernation. I want to put another question against that What are we, and what can we do?

I was talking to the Community Relations Council in the North and I was arguing that culture has a fundamental role to play in reconstructing a society (and indeed in society as a whole), and some one asked, what is culture? I replied that it was what people make and what people do. Some of that making and doing will be in ways that everybody understands, and using a language that is directly understood as being art. But also I think, how people lead their lives, that too is cultural. People are already participants in a cultural process, just by being alive and making decisions, and acting upon those decisions. And they are not just consumers of cultural products.

It is right to say, What do we do? Once you get down to that level of questioning you construct the reality of political systems, which, in the context of extremism, in Northern Ireland, or in the Middle East, comes to the fundamential of What am I? It is happening in Eastern Europe as well. And what does it mean to say, I am Irish? I come from a sort of Catholic nationalist background, what does it mean? Those are just words. All that can really and properly explored, without damaging other people (and that's a key point), through culture. You can then make artefacts which will contain those values.

The Irish Museum of Modern Art is at the Royal Hospital Kilmainham, Dublin 8, Ireland.
Telephone +353-1-6718666.
Admission is free, with varied charges
for special exhibitions

David Rose, a critic and historian, directed an arts centre in West Cork, Ireland, for eighteen years. He is a regular writer in the Cork Citizen, and continues to curate exhibitions

Documenta X

Catherine David, Artistic Director, Documenta X, recorded in conference 27.02.1997, at the Goethe Institute, London.

(Editor's note: due to the poor quality of the recording errors and slippages may have occurred in the transcript.)

CD. This Documenta has not been organised under the Flag, meaning that we can't look at the world as before. as US / German or as a soft-edged cultural constellation. So given all the levels, we have not tried to answer all questions. But how we put work on exhibition, with this perspective, with the whole perspective, which is not huge. For the team it was very necessary to think about the global context of Documenta; trying to figure out where we were, where we would like to go, knowing we are not magicians, and we are not a simple voice - we are asking sometimes for answers, just trying to see what could be relevant, what could be possible. What could be the period path for aesthetic practices under the frame of progressive attitudes.

So I will go on with the notion of the Retroperspective - again, it's not the Retrospective. To deal with all that happened after 1945 is too much, and isn't necessarily to do with the frame of Documenta. We tried to exorcise practices by the first Documenta generation who were born immediately after or at the very end of the war, and practices which were developed in the mid sixties, which were developed under the new meaning of critical art - the configuring of the market - which was very concerned with cultural practices on the political level. I know some people are disturbed by this sort of exploration, so we make some distinctions about critical art. We can distinguish on three levels the level of agit-prop, the reactive art, to a problem or an accident of nature, an incident. The critical art developed into the middle and late fifties; the making of art specified as critical practice. Again, the criticism of the system of making art, the polemicists we try to work with this, which would be the third level of critical practice. This was very strong in the 1970s, trying to articulate the cultural areas; meaning that, when you deal with architecture you also deal with social problems. When you deal with the history of language you also deal with the whole of culture. Speaking like this is very simplistic, but it is also the best way of introducing names like Marcel Broodthaers, International Histories, Oyvind Fahlstrom.

So Retroperspective means we are trying to question again, to make a fresh start, using models which are not an obvious source of inspiration for young artists, but represent a very strong genealogy. The simple fact is these works are still questioning us, and that says a lot about their relevance. The fact that we need to look at them. The attitudes of post '45 are explored in Retroperspective and are in the book. '45, '60 - it also shows the impossibility of Documenta to do justice to local social problems. In the book you can be much more subtle and can work with many more complex articulations. As regards the walls, Documenta has some real museum and classical exhibition spaces, so it has not been necessary to take the risk of destroying the nature of the work by..we have also the problems of sources outside the exhibition which are supposed to be apart from Retroperspective, of the containers which are supposed to... There has been a space specially built which is called the Documenta Halle. The advantage we had from the last Documenta was what we saw from the beginning. We knew from that in advance what we couldn't do with it (laughter). We should try therefore to use it as a meeting place, a discussion space, it will be a forum. We have of course works which have to do with networks and with new communications, tragedies, and a continuing forum called *One Hundred Days - One Hundred Guests.*

There is the park, which is very nice in summer and might be used for special events. The Parcours has some works in the sculpture garden which are not transforming the area (shows slides). There are works on site which are not transforming the area, so we kept the best, or the worst, and that which we couldn't move (laughter) The Kilometre by Walter de Maria, or the *7000 Oaks* by Joseph Beuys. Many, many works which could be monsters, but make a kind of place for visiting different moments of art; sculpture developing from the '60s on. So we will have some projects which will be removed at the end of Documenta, also knowing what the city of Kassel doesn't want to buy, or like what we like.

In these conditions I think it's good to work from projects that can be removed, and which relate at certain times to what you can say, what you want. So to know a monument which is not a monument, or just a few projects..can we have some light now? (Finishes slide presentation) The idea for this Documenta, apart from the Retroperspective, was to try to face the changes in contemporary practices - in trying to make physical a part of them. Again, many practices I am interested in are highly dangerous for not being ridiculous in the normal frame of Documenta.

We try to find possible spaces for a number of highly interesting artists. This Documenta is using very different spaces it has - meaning, the book, the space of the discourse, the discussion, the space of debate. This Documenta is also using the real spaces, and TV channels, the spaces which are not the immediate wall, the confrontational space. For the rest, we felt it was important to emphasise the many contemporary practices; works, and I will be brief, because I don't think medium distinctions are ideal these days. Works which are in a moment when we are facing in a way ..more obliged to face a uni-dimension, mega dimension, mega because it's **Mega**.

It's not hard to understand Mega is a dimension without scale, without real possibility. In the end mega is the only tool for measuring Mega with a capital M, and nothing else. We are highly interested, especially of course in the young generation, by whose practices, attitudes, corruptions, are trying to

Peter Kogler: **Tapete** in the Documenta Hall, Documenta X, Kassel, 1997 Cv/VAR Archive

oppose this Mega dimension - those territories, meaning a medium as space, and of course the occupation of this space, is very complex, subjective - inter-subjective, articulation of very precise, very specific situations.

For me it is much more important to understand what many young artists are doing, than trying to - if it's a picture, if it's a video, it's an edition, it's a performance, it's a book page, and so on. I think you can play with that, if it doesn't take you too long. And in the different buildings we try to articulate more positions than themes.

It's always difficult to talk of technical or practical problems, even the political ones, so it's obvious with the museum space that you have some imperatives, apart from placements of works which are due to unavoidable, practical problems. We tried to organize the ideas around the technical changes to the production from the mid '60s on, and of course to articulate major historical works with new ones. And I think that, better than the big discourses, one way of integrating the major statements from the '60s, which is not European but which is Western, is like a Third World one, an African space. It's not too difficult to foreground works which articulate this condition.

I try to work, not with the notion of freshness, that is not necessarily good for art. When it was interesting we worked with works that had a very complex history or theme, trying to articulate different distances, different moments. You have artists who worked with long distances, with drawing; a very practical but very complex cultural medium. A medium in a way of all the disabilities, one of the most experimental mediums.

And also to make visible and conscious all the different generations; concerning the vision of artists who are not really young people - sometimes even old (laughter), not just because it's the last Documenta, but trying to make a statement of what art could be.

I guess some people would be very surprised by the old ones, many devoted to image practices, and the young ones who are mostly involved with phenomenology - who are trained to read many things happening in our inter-subjective relationships; the way you are differing in spaces and so on. And people from West and Non-West, all articulated more or less. It's not a theme, it's more a contact - more or less.

If you put together young artists from altogether different cultural areas and knowing that probably your contact is strong enough and tough enough, and unavoidable enough, to bring into the West certain generational attitudes.

I guess in Singapore, in Sao Paolo, in Berlin, you have certain common attitudes, certain emergencies you have to face, which are certain specific reactions of one generation. And it's working out, in a very difficult way, this problem; of putting together practices which will move on and develop. Very different cultural areas are not so obvious to juxtapose without taking care of the cultural formations, of possible emergencies. So working on this project we have all sorts of incidents and accidents which have to do with the relativation of practices.

The director of Documenta X Opens out to questions and engages in general discussion with the audience.

Artistic Director, Catherine David trained in Literature, Linguistics and Art History in Paris, where she has been curator at the Jeu de Paume and lecturer at the Ecole de Paris

Silver Image

The Collection of The Royal Photographic Society Bath Interview with Curator Pamela Roberts, recorded 27.10.93

Cv/VAR. Who started the Royal Photographic Society, and was its motivating force?

PR. It was formed in 1853, as an offshoot of the Royal Society of Arts. The motivating force was Roger Fenton, who was the first secretary of the society and his work is one of our biggest collections of photography, we have about seven hundred and fifty photographs in all. Fenton had been over to Paris, he'd worked there with photographers such as Gustave Le Gray and Henri Le Secq. In 1882 they set up Le Societe Heliographique, and he was impressed by the fact that there was a separate photographic society, so, he came back and set up a similar sort of thing in the UK. It was also stimulated by The Great Exhibition at Crystal Palace in London 1851, where photography was shown en masse for the first time. There was also a large photographic exhibition held at the Royal Society of Arts at the end of 1852, and from the interest generated, Fenton called a meeting of like-minded individuals, to form a Photographic Society.

Did they have any stated ideals or agenda?

Their ideals were to advance the art and science of photography (reads) 'The object of the Photographic Society is the promotion of the Art and Science of Photography by the interchange of thought and experience among Photographers, and it is hoped this object may, to some considerable extent, be effected by the periodical meetings of the Society.' At the first meeting it was decided they would establish a photographic journal. The first issue was in March 1853, and is still being published. They would have annual exhibitions of work of their members and establish a darkroom in London. The first base they had was in Russell Square.

What was their funding?

They weren't funded and never have been. This is one of the problems of the RPS. Fenton was a friend of Prince Albert, who was very interested in photography and had a darkroom at Windsor Castle. Fenton had worked with Prince Albert prior to 1853, on things like Adult Education Classes; like the Working Men's Association in Camden Town. This was set up to assist working men's appreciation of the arts; stonemasonry, crafts, and so on. Albert was very interested in these philanthropic, educational projects, and he and Queen Victoria were the Society's first Patrons. He came to all the meetings and was really quite involved. However we did not get the Royal addition to our title until 1894.

Has the RPS always been in Bath?

No, we moved here in 1979. The society moved around London and gradually acquired bigger and bigger premises as the Collection grew; first in Russell Square and then at Prince's Gate, Kensington, in the 1960s and '70s. That building was sold to the Iranian Embassy, the one which was later stormed by the SAS. When the lease was up for renewal at the South Audley Street site at Hyde Park, they decided to form a National Centre for Photography, with a study centre based on our own Collection, which is phenomenal. At that point they decided to move out of London to Bath, and opened here in 1980.

In the early days of the RPS the members were the experimenters with the medium. They were scientists and artists, a lot of them had an artistic background. Fenton was a painter, Rejlander as well, and many of them earned their living as artists. The society was seen as a meeting place for new inventions the idea was to bring in your research, say, having reached a certain stage with a coated glass negative, but with something not quite right, and people could contribute to it. It was like a think tank. All the cameras were pretty big, compared with what we've got now.

Fenton had a photographic van converted from an old vintner's carriage, which he stripped out and painted white to reflect the heat of the Crimea. It was kitted out internally as a darkroom. Fenton worked with 20″ x 16″ glass negatives, which slid into the back of a camera with a 22″ x 18″ span. So he worked with a huge camera to achieve a great depth of field.

At the Victoria and Albert Museum they have the four feet square negatives in their collection, dating from the late 1850s. These were sheets of glass which had to be hand coated just before exposure. It wasn't something that could be done back in your own darkroom, you had to take them onto the field. There are letters from Fenton in the Crimea describing how they had to be out by seven in the morning. After that the light became too strong and it was phenomenally hot. They were working in temperatures of 110 degrees, plus there was the dust. You coated your negative with collodion, which is a very sticky mixture, like nail varnish, and every speck of dust would stick to it, as well as the sweat of the photographers.

These conditions have all been documented, as well as the rampant cholera. Fenton used gutta-percha trays which melted in the heat. Then you have to look at the amazing quality of the pictures the prints were contacts of the 20″ x 16″ plate negatives, as there were no enlargements in those dys until the 1860s, when solar enlarging came in.

In the Crimea Fenton was working with three cameras; a large format camera at 18″ x 14″, a smaller camera, probably about 10″ x 8″, and a stereo camera, setting up different shots. He was commissioned by Agnew's in London, to go out on their behalf and photograph the campaign, and to bring the prints back, which were then sold in sets; either mounted in albums, or sold as loose prints. Agnew's wanted a variety of formats at a variety of prices, so they could sell as many as they could.

The pioneer of photography, Henry Fox Talbot, was based near Bath at Lacock Abbey, and the RPS has a major holding of his works. Did he use glass negatives too?

No, this was before glass came in. He worked with paper negatives. Nicephore Niepce had invented Heliogravure, which was an image etched on a pewter plate. He then worked with Louis-Jaques Mande, to develop what became the Daguerrotype. Niepce died and Daguerre took over, some would say, taking all the credit as well. Daguerre and Niepce invented a unique image, if you wanted another Daguerreotype of yourself, you had to go back to the studio and sit again. Fox Talbot invented the negative, from which you can get an infinite number of positives. That was made on paper, and therefore you got the grain of the paper coming through. The image was saturated into the paper.

Talbot started by coating the paper with a light sensitive solution putting a leaf on, a piece of lace, or something that sunlight could pass through, exposing it. But the light sensitive solution would darken, which was a problem. What Talbot discovered, with a lot of help from John Herschel, was how to fix it. That was the important thing; that he had control of the darkening action. From that stage you could then take your paper negative, wax it to make it more translucent, then sandwich it with another piece of coated paper put the two together in a printing frame out in the sun, and in that way you got your positive image.

People had to sit rigidly still for several minutes for a portrait?

Yes. Initially his exposure times were very long, but as he found out more about solutions, he could make more rapidly reacting mixtures. Then there were better lenses. His first cameras were tiny little mouse hole contraptions, which eventually progressed to bigger cameras,

longer focal lengths, and more rapid exposures.

And what about the Hill and Adamson photographs ?

They were slightly later. Talbot put a patent on his invention, and thereafter, everybody who wanted to use it in a professional way had to pay him rather large amounts of money. But that didn't apply to amateurs, nor did it apply in Scotland. Hill and Adamson were based in Edinburgh. David Octavius Hill was a painter, the brothers John and Robert Adamson were both chemists, but Robert got together with David Octavius Hill, who wanted to use photographs as an aide-memoire for his painting a large tableau of the Free Presbytarian Meeting in Scotland, that contained some five hundred people. He thought if he could get them all in individual groups, he could record each one for the painted portrait.

Hill, therefore, would do the composition, the lighting and the dramatic effect, and Adamson would do the chemical side of it. What happened was that Hill became more obsessed with the photography side of it than the painting. After they'd recorded a lot of groups, they started the first real documentary exploration They had plans to go round Scotland to record the life of the villages. They went to Newhaven and photographed the fishing community there, which is the most wonderful series. We have about four hundred Hill and Adamsons here. They were going to go to the Highlands and Lowlands, and document the various ways of life, when Adamson died at an early age,

An Unknown Woman
Salt print circa 1845 Attrib. Rev Calvert Richard Jones (1802-77)
Coll. Cv/VAR Archive

possibly brought on by the chemicals he used. He was slightly tubercular, but the horrible stuff he worked with didn't help, such as potassium cyanide. Hill's subsequent partnerships never gelled in the same way.

Were these early experiments preserved by the photographers' families, and in what state did they come to you?

Yes, by and large. The chemical state is amazingly good. To go back to Prince Albert; he started collecting photographs to chart its progress over fourteen years. If you go through our minute books for the 1850s, Gustave Le Gray brought over some of his seascapes and left them in London, though they later disappeared, as we don't have them any more. By 1923 the new president of the society, John Dudley Johnston decided he would give a speech about the society's famous past, and the photographers who had been involved. Johnston went to the archives, such as they were, to look at what was there, and all there was were a hundred framed pictures from a variety of people, that had been presented to the society. So he decided he would start avidly collecting photographs, forming what is probably the first collection of photography in the world.

He also started researching the past history, going to the descendants of the photographers, who were not far enough removed to have split the collections. So at this point, all Fenton's material came in, over the next ten years. Also the Julia Margaret Cameron collection, of about seven hundred and eighty photographs. Regarding Fox Talbot, in 1935 his last living descendant Matilda Fox Talbot, who was unmarried, with no children to pass the collection on to, gave Lacock, the abbey and the whole village, to the National Trust. However, she decided to give some of the photographs to the two big collections, the RPS and the Science Museum. Humphrey Barclay, who was the curator at the Science Museum, and Dudley Johnston, were invited to Lacock to help themselves.

We have photographs of that visit and the Fox Talbot calotypes are fixed to a board with drawing pins; hundreds of them all around Lacock Abbey, which would make dealers weep with despair. But I don't think much got lost. The Science Museum took six thousand, we took a much smaller number, but an example of everything.

Talbot didn't just invent the negative, he went on to work with something called photoglyphic engraving, from which, later on, photogravure developed. Our curator took examples of everything to show what Fox Talbot had been doing over a thirty year period. We have about three hundred images; negatives and various positives showing, for instance, how he tried to stop the photographs fading, doing everything possible to stop the yellowing of the image, or its disappearance. A lot of our Talbots are covered in a shellac varnish.

Could you still print off the original paper negatives?

Yes, it's been done. In the '60s and '70s people here did print off the originals. We now make an internegative, it's called a surrogate negative. This negative can be printed, so you don't damage the original. We have a portrait of Constance Talbot, his wife, which we think is the first portrait, from February 1840. It's dated on the back. Before that it was inanimate objects, a lot of still life, and the famous window which is now up at the National Museum of Photography, Film and Television in Bradford. It is wonderful, a beautiful blue-brown colour. It has faded over the last hundred and fifty years. The chemicals were impure then. Silver nitrate would have other bits and pieces in it, and there are chemical reactions which are very hard to predict. Some of the material is pale yellow, others purple-blue.

So you keep a watchful eye on things?

We try, but technical monitoring can't be done with the human eye, you have to do densitometer readings to see what's happening. The originals are kept in acid free boxes, on metal shelving in a dark room, and are not often exhibited.

The Royal Photographic Society is at Milsom Street, Bath, Somerset, BA1 1DN.
Telephone 01225 462841. Fax 01225 448688.
Research enquiries only

Theatre Museum

Introduction by Tiffany Black*

The Theatre Museum, situated in Covent Garden, is in the heart of London's Theatre Land, and was opened on April 23rd 1987. After many years of spirited campaigning this at last gave recognition to the extraordinary collections begun by Mrs Gabrielle Enthoven, and donated to the Victoria and Albert Museum in 1925. Since that time they have been greatly enlarged upon, and now span the performing arts to include; theatre, ballet and dance, circus, music hall, opera to mime, puppetry, rock and pop music. The Theatre Museum has a permanent exhibition and two smaller galleries; the Irving Gallery and the Gielgud Gallery, where changing exhibitions are shown.

The museum houses a theatre showing a variety of productions which are also used for lectures and workshops. Extensive research collections and a library are open to the public, offering access to books and bibiographic information on thousands of actors, designers, directors and writers, prompt scripts, press cuttings and photographic files, covering 19th and 20th century performers and productions. Alongside this the museum stages a number of exhibition related events throughout the year, and offers a licensed restaurant and small shop.

Leela Meinertas, archivist of the Theatre Museum, in conversation with Sarah Batiste. Interview recorded 5.12.1989

SB. This museum is the basis of a very large collection, how did it all start?
LM. The Theatre Museum was officially founded in 1974. Prior to that time there were collections of theatre material at the Victoria and Albert Museum books in the library, models and set designs in the print department, costumes in the costume department, and so on. In 1974 they all came together, including collections from other bodies which were interested in developing a centre for theatre art the British Theatre Museum Association, Friends of the Museum of Theatre Arts, The Society of Theatre Research.

At the same time design collections came to us one from the Arts Council of Great Britain, and the second from the British Council. They had been formed as touring exhibitions which went all over the world. In some cases the models were remakes and some of the designs were redrawn, but a large percentage was original. And since neither the Arts Council nor the British Council were primarily collecting bodies, but exhibiting ones, we were the logical home. There are some marvellously interesting things in the collection, for instance, work by Derek Jarman, who one associates more with film direction and production.
You have a portfolio here of his set designs?
This is for Jazz Calendar, a ballet at Covent Garden in January '68. As well as designs we keep backup material posters, press cuttings, programmes, photo-

graphs, which are useful for researchers. The usual thing about set and costume designs is that what one sees in studies isn't necessarily what appears on stage. It's a very precarious business, not like Haut Couture, where the design for a dress or a suit is final, it can change during a performance. But even with someone like Derek Jarman, who has a very abstract approach to design; on the whole his designs can be read, so the costumier knows from his drawings exactly what he wants. Nowadays British theatre designers' work can often look like works of art, and in many cases there isn't even a note given to say what something is made out of. Here Derek Jarman describes the setting for Wednesday's Child in Jazz Calendar ...*Pearls about ten feet, sack at least twelve feet, with silver dust to catch light...* The information is restricted to what the set will look like. With younger designers, they now tell you where the actors or dancerswill move, or how they will do things, which always used to be the province of the director or choreographer. It's interesting that the designers are now taking a more directorial role in productions.

I imagine the designers see the thing as a coherent whole?

Absolutely. Whereas thirty years ago the designer would have had a meeting with the director to find out what was wanted, I think now we're coming away from director's theatre and more into designer's theatre. It depends very much who you're working for. The designers working for subsidised companies have great advantages they have their own workshops, their own studios, and can be relatively extravagant. One of the most exciting current designers is Philip Prowse, who is based at the Glasgow Citizens Theatre, where the funds are miniscule. He designs and directs, and is equally talented in both fields. His productions, in my opinion, are always utterly spectacular.

Derek Jarman has recently been designing for Rock Groups?

He has done a Harvey Goldsmith's concert for the Pet Shop Boys at Wembley last summer. Again, when you go to a rock concert, be it Madonna, Michael Jackson, Elton John, there is never really any mention of the designer. We don't think of it being designed but as an event. Pop is an area we are getting interested in, particularly stage costumes, where performers are notorious for their stage wear like Elton John, Kiss, Brian Eno, Sandy Shaw's dresses.

We have all Adam Ant's costumes. We also have a Blondie dress, and a Mick Jagger jumpsuit, among others. They're genuine stage designs, sometimes rather badly put together, but they are there to create an effect. Designers can also range enormously in their method of working David Hockney's sets are like his paintings; we have a model for a set designed by Howard Hodgkin, and there's no question it's a Hodgkin when you see it, it's very painterly.

A designer like Julia Trevelyan Oman is meticulous to the most extraordinary degree. She did The Nutcracker for the Royal Festival Ballet, and one can be certain that each interior and costume was researched thoroughly down to the smallest prop. We have a volume for Brief Lives it's like a filofax with every minutely detail recorded, it's almost like an encyclopaedia or a mosaic, there's nothing arbitrary or out of place. Our collections go right up to the present day, and last year we acquired a model and costume designs by Yolanda Sonnabend for Covent Garden's new production of Swan Lake.

We have here a gouache painting of a figure in a black costume scattered with silver dust. It's amazing and very typically Sonnabend.

Very. The previous production of Swan Lake at Covent Garden had been the Sadlers Wells production designed by Lesley Hurry, which ran since the '40s. From that we have the costume designs and some details. Yolanda Sonnabend is usually associated with modern dance, so it is fascinating to see her approach to classical ballet, which is incredibly rich and sensuous.

One of your favourite designers is Gladys Calthrop?

Now everyone has heard of Noel Coward, and will be able to rattle off dozens of his plays and songs. A Coward production like The Vortex shows a certain kind of style of the'20s and '30s with which he is so closely identified. Gladys Calthrop was the woman behind the man, in a way. She designed The Vortex, his first play, at the Everyman Theatre, Hampstead, in 1924. She was actually an artist, trained at the Slade, before embarking on stage design, after meeting Coward in the early 1920s. She working with Coward virtually throughout his career. He acknowledged her as a friend,

but never much as a designer. There is no appraisal of her work in his diaries, nor in the biographies, but we have an enormous collection of nearly everything she did. For instance, she designed every costume for Cavalcade at Drury Lane 1931, of which there were hundreds. She did it all herself, designed the sets and the costumes for most of his productions.

We have reviews and photographs from the first presentation of The Vortex, and nothing was written about what it looked like - it was the same with Cavalcade. People were more interested in the content of Coward than in the visual aspect. Perhaps there was a passing reference to the spectacular costumes. I assume she must have been a very private person who never gave interviews.

It's interesting how some designers seem to fade.

The nature of design has changed. In the '20s and the '30s designers worked more like stylists, and in quite an ordinary way; I suppose in a similar way that stylists now dress commercials. Today's theatre designer is a completely different animal.

---

* **The Theatre Museum** in Covent Garden was the UK's National Museum of the Performing Arts. It was a branch of the UK's National Museum of Applied Arts, the Victoria and Albert Museum. It closed in 2007, and has now been replaced by new galleries at the V&A's main site in South Kensington. *Source: Wikipedia*

NatWest Art Collection

Rosemary Harris, Curator, NatWest Art Collection, interviewed 11.02.1997, at the launch of The Lothbury Gallery, London.

Cv/VAR. You put this exhibition together?
R H. That's correct.
But was the collection already here?
The collection was owned by NatWest, yes.
Do you have anything to do with the collecting of pictures?
Yes.
So do you buy from the major West End galleries, or international dealers? How do you pick and choose the collection?
Because it's contemporary British art, it's mainly the dealers and artists within London really. So it involves visiting artist's studios, exhibitions, and people also send things into me.
So you purchase directly from the artist?
Sometimes, if the artist doesn't have a dealer; it depends on the artist, what the set up is really.
Is there any particular policy, thematic or..?
When I arrived here a year ago from the Tate, one of the things I had to do was look at the collection, bring it together and see what was in it. What seemed to be the two main strains was post-war British painting, with an emphasis on fine contemporary work. So that was the focus that I felt we should build on - the post-war British - but also buy emerging younger British artists who are of interest.
Yes, I noticed Callum Innes.
That's right, and Antoni Malinowski,

Mark Francis, Simon Mills. But then we bought Bert Irvin, who is an established artist, who fits in with works that we have by John Hoyland as well.
Are there limitations here in the sense of what you can do in displays? Would you do installation works for instance?
At some point we might do, we'd have to consider each particular piece. To me, what the space calls out for is sculpture; clear all the screens out of the way and put sculpture out.
That might be part of the programme?
We might borrow some sculpture, not necessarily go out and buy it in.
What's coming up next?
The NatWest Prize For Art. Eleven finalists' work will be displayed here in May. We've changed it, relaunched it this year to look at what we're purchasing for the Prize For Art. Painting is terribly exciting now, and a thing we've got to support traditional skills used in an innovative way, that's the key. It's innovative, but celebrating painting. Not as a contrast or challenge to The Turner Prize at the Tate, but I think as a positive painting experience. Someone for instance like Gary Hume, who is shortlisted for The Turner Prize, but equally could be in for the Natwest Prize.

The Lothbury Gallery located on the ground floor of the NatWest Group Head Office at 41 Lothbury, London EC2. Telephone 020 7726 1642/1643

Tate Modern in Construction

Interviews with Dawn Austwick (DA) and Jeremy Lewison (JL), recorded 6.03.1997

DA. (dealing with visitor enquiry)
I'm afraid it's closed today...we've discovered on site, every day people just turn up, it's amazing. The level of interest is incredible.
Cv/VAR. Looking up at the building, it's so big, and yet, probably for years, they walked by Bankside and didn't notice it.
DA. Well I worked over the river, on the other side, for eight years in Puddle Dock, just along from the Mermaid Theatre, and I remember once looking across at this huge building and thinking, oh, I wonder what that is? That was the only time in eight years.
Extraordinary, and yet now it's got this title it seems so appropriate.
It's amazing isn't it? It's incredible. There was a television programme on Monday about the City of London Boys School, and they filmed visitors on that side of the river looking across here with the building in the background, and they were talking about 'it's wonderful, because it's right opposite where the new Tate Gallery's going to be.' It's extraordinary the way it's gone from an invisible landmark to a visible one. And yet it's exactly the same.
What's your role?
My basic brief is to deliver for the gallery, as near as damn it, what they want in terms of vision, within the constraints of budget and time. So I suppose I have to make sure we raise the money,

and that we raise the money in the right sequence; that we get the building built, and that we do it to the highest standards that we require.
You are involved in getting pledges from the various bodies?
In a way, yes. I have a finger in every pie, so that the way we structure the project is, if you like, I orchestrate as project director and then we have a building team, we have a fundraising team, we have an advocacy team, a communications team, which is where Erica comes in *(Erica Bolton of Bolton & Quinn Ltd)*, on the PR side. We have a project support team and we have an embryonic programme team. I dig and delve into all of them; so I will get involved in some fundraising, in the public sector fundraising - so the National Lottery work we've done, I led. If there's a particular target donor that I might have some coincidental relationship with, or whatever, or it's a prototype that's involved with them, but no more than anyone else in a sense. Where I'm very involved with fundraising is in the strategic direction, in terms of - what is the time that we need to raise funds and review progress? And managing that within the framework of the whole project.
How secure is a pledge? Is the Lottery funding solid?
Well I suppose, at my most conservative, I would say that no money is secure until it's in our bank account, and there's a hierarchy of how secure you think it is. If you take Lottery money, even that could be revoked technically, if the Lottery collapsed, and we might not get

the rest of our money, though we've already had some.

But the Tate has to feel happy before it signs building contracts?

Yes, that is correct. The total project will cost us £130 million, of which we have secured £100 million. Now we couldn't say that that entire £100 million is without any risk whatsoever, because that £100 million will include pledges from donors who will say, 'we'll give it to you over five years.'

They set the terms?

Yes, and we might have had installment one and installment two, and then there's three, four and five to come. It's conceivable, just as in any business arrangement, that they could go belly up.

But you have contingency plans, life rafts?

The contingency is that we have sufficient money in the bank to deliver, and sufficient irons in the fire should some fall through. We don't actually count a pledge as firm until it's all written and documented, and there's a contractual agreement. Some of our donors just write us a cheque on account. For example there are a number of people who have said they will give us money, some have said how much, others simply promised to give. None of that counts against our total.

You have to go on and on, raising funds?

It basically moves from starting an opening negotiation, and that doesn't count in your calculations, it's just part of the target that you've got to achieve. Then you think your percentage evaluations of success increases as you go through.

An offer from someone that's a verbal offer, from one source you would say that's ninety five percent secure; from another source you would say, hang on, that's only fifty percent secure. All those sorts of calculations go into that line of thinking.

It's complicated.

It is. It feels like juggling different balls, and it changes all the time. One of the real mistakes you can make in a project like this is believing you can run it like a computer programme, because the situation changes from day to day and week to week. The fundraising might be full steam ahead for six months and then hit a problem. And you never know where it might come from.

But if you're looking to open in the Year 2000 and you have two years to complete the building, and then to fit it out?

Yes, the construction programme is twenty three months, from summer '97 to summer '99.

The architects Herzog and de Meuron have done their job?

They've done the bulk of it, but they stay on site through construction as well. The majority of the work of the design team, in design terms, will be completed by the summer, obviously. There are elements of fit-out that we're not doing yet; for example, the detail of precisely how the educational facilities will look. I mean we know where the lavatories are, where the rooms are, but how we configure those spaces, we will actually leave till a little later.

The gallery spaces are where?

Levels three, four and five. If I start you

at the bottom level one is the entrance area and combines the Turbine Hall, which if you look at those black and white photos, that's it. It is an astonishing space.

You're retaining the drama of that aspect?

Absolutely, it's even emptier now. It's five hundred feet long, about one hundred feet wide, and one hundred and twenty feet tall.

Who spotted it first - Nick Serota?

No, actually. This is mythology that predates me. It is said somebody called Francis Carnwath found it, who was the previous administrative director of the Tate. He was sent off to find sites and came back one day to say, 'I've found this extraordinary place, come and look at it.' On level one the Turbine Hall in effect becomes a rather extraordinary covered street.

Like an arcade?

That kind of downgrades it a little bit, but, absolutely, in that it could be open when the gallery's closed. It could be a grand meeting place. You can get to it from stage one, which is the western entrance. If you're coming from the north you come from a level above.

Examining the plans

This is looking at the northern entrance, which is on level two. This is level one, the main west entrance. You come down a huge ramp that brings you down to the bottom of the building. All our ticketing and information will be in this area. The whole of this area is the main gallery building, including the schools area, conveniences, shop, all down here. If you come from the north, you come in either side of the chimney, across onto a bridge which runs over, and either come down by the lift or the stairs. In the long run there'll be an entrance from the south, where the big gates are presently. This is an auditorium, cafe and bar area, a film seminar room, the loading bay area and back of house facilities. Here is level three, the first area of galleries with circulation all in the central area, vertically. Escalators run all the way up, and the central staircase. This is a concourse area in effect. The gallery space is basically two wings on each floor; level four and five are all gallery spaces.

A considerable space then?

Yes, we get more than at Millbank at present. Whether we do level four will depend on how much money we raise; over £130 million, or we'll hold it as a shell.

The excitement of it is what you'd hope to make work?

Absolutely. It more than doubles our display facility, which is fantastic. The soaring tower in the long run, will have a high speed lift to a viewing platform. The light beam sits on the top, which first and foremost creates double length spaces in these galleries, and brings daylight in from either side.

The big problem, and to avoid a split, must be shifting visitors to the new gallery from Millbank. You need a regeneration process of the South Bank area to persuade people to come down here?

Well I think it's very interesting, because if you actually walk along the South Bank of the river, starting say at County

Hall, you can go right down past Tower Bridge to Butler's Wharf, and you can trace pockets of development all the way up. Then there's the vacant site that the Opera House is going into, Hays Wharf Galleria and the London Dungeon. Southwark Cathedral and the Clink area, Southwark Bridge, The Globe and us. So actually there's quite an interesting development already, of, if you like, cultural attractions.

That's one way of moving down the river, what about going to St.Paul's Cathedral and coming across?

That's the other element. In terms of tourism there's an east-west axis, then north-south. The north-south axis for Bankside goes from St.Paul's, the Museum of London and The Barbican across to The Tate at Bankside and The Globe. For that to develop, and I think that the Tate is going to succeed in terms of its visitors regardless; for London as a whole at the moment there's too much tourism focused in the West End. Everybody agrees it's congested; the focus of London First and the London Tourist Board is to develop new clusters. To get that north-south one happening we need the footbridge, in my view. And what that does is it opens up a series of different pedestrian experiences, which we don't currently have. The great thing about the river bank is you can walk the whole way. There's a project to deliver a new foot bridge across the river which we're involved in. Fosters Associates have just won that, subject to a millennium bid.

Has the Millennium Project at Greenwich affected you?

Our fundraising from private sources is much more focused on individuals. Unlike Greenwich we're not looking to the corporate sector to provide us with capital funding, though clearly when the gallery opens we will seek to work with our corporate partners and new ones before the year 2000. But in terms of the capital programme our absolute major focus has been the Lottery and Public sector; individuals and Trust organisations, and that's a pretty recognised route for capital funding.

Jeremy Lewison (JL), Acting Keeper of the Modern Collection, Tate Britain, Millbank.

Cv/VAR. Moving the whole modern collection to Bankside, which I assume includes post-war British...

JL. No, you've already made two assumptions which are incorrect. First of all, we're not moving the modern collection. The collection is a central resource which can be displayed on any one of four sites Millbank, Bankside, Liverpool and St.Ives, and if there's any one place where the collection is based, it's our new store at Southwark. From the year 2000, when Bankside opens, we will be displaying there British and Foreign art - or art from around the world, if you like, from 1900 onwards. And at Millbank we will be showing British art from 16th century to the present day. 20th century art will be shown in both sites.

Will the visiting public move comfortably between the two Tates?

The visitor who wants to see 'The

Story of British Art', will come to Millbank; it's obviously a gallery which has a specialist feeling in that respect. Areas of foreign art from time to time will be shown at Millbank, but only as they illuminate a particular aspect of British art that we may want to focus on. So, for example, when you're doing a St.Ives display you may want to bring in some abstract expressionist art, to give a cliched example. Those people who want specifically to concentrate on 20th century art, and they want to see a full international range of it, will go to Bankside. And there will be some people who go between the two. There have been suggestions that maybe there would be a riverbus service at one point. There is talk, for example, of gaining permission for some kind of pier outside Millbank, and we already have a landing stage outside Bankside, though it needs rebuilding.

How long would it take to get from Millbank to Bankside?

Ten minutes in a car - through traffic, fifteen minutes. On a riverbus, ten minutes. It's only four bridges along. Inevitably some people might turn up at Millbank thinking they were coming to see the 20th century modern collection, including foreign art, but we would hope that our pre-publicity would be sufficiently good to avoid that most of the time. But we are keen to connect the two galleries in that sense, so people can easily go from one to the other.

How does this change the exhibition programme? At the Tate Millbank the blockbuster exhibitions such as Cézanne in 1996 have attracted major audiences. Will that still continue on both sites? A major show at Millbank, and a major show at Bankside - it's a lot of work, investment and expense.

We will need to continue to put on exhibitions which we estimate will be popular, but at the same time, we feel there is a good art historical reason for doing it. And the same applies in both institutions. As far as Bankside is concerned the exhibitions programme will have to pay for itself, so while we will have some exhibitions which will be very, very popular, they will subsidize the other exhibitions which may not be so popular, but we feel are important to do. The same will apply to the Tate Gallery of British Art.

We are currently looking into what kinds of programmes, and what sort of variety of programmes we should be doing. We will be doing exhibitions on a large scale, and mid-scale exhibitions which we haven't previously been able to do. At the moment our exhibitions are in twelve rooms; in the future we will do some exhibitions at twelve rooms, and at the same time will do exhibitions which are six rooms, or four rooms, so that we can focus in on particular areas over a brief period of an artist's work, or even do exhibitions of artists who we feel we couldn't financially justify on a large scale, but feel their work should be shown, so we'll do it on a smaller scale.

We know that in recent years the public has woken up to contemporary art, and it is now a tremendous draw for a number of reasons, providing the case that you could probably use the new space at Bankside for very fresh art. Would you be thinking of that?

We are thinking of not only displaying the collection, and works of a 20th century historic nature, but we are also exploring possibilities of doing projects with artists, and dedicating some galleries to contemporary art exhibits. Here at Millbank we have the Art Now room, which we would continue to maintain. We will continue to do the Turner Prize display here, and we will continue to find space in the exhibition programme to do contemporary shows of British art.

So there'll be a rich diet of exhibitions, which will include historic and contemporary work on both sites. And in terms of the display of the collection, on both sites again, we'll be dedicating a certain amount of space to contemporary work. More perhaps at Bankside than at Millbank.

It would be weighted in that direction then?

Not because we feel it's more suitable for Bankside, but we will have an increase of about 25% of space at Millbank over what we currently have, for the display of the collection. We're creating new galleries downstairs which will release space upstairs for the collection. But that is going to spread evenly over the whole range of the collection from Elizabethan times to the present day. So there will be considerable pressure on space for contemporary art at Bankside. It is our view to see British contemporary art within the context of art made in other countries.

With visiting artists from other countries?

When you say visiting artists, we could do projects with artists of other nationalities than Britain at Bankside, yes. And there is work by non-British artists already in the collection.

There's a broader art-historical question nagging here; coming to the Tate at Millbank one enjoys floating between the Constables and the Rothkos, and making connections between now and then. Will one be able to do that at Bankside, or will it only be the modern, new and contemporary? Maybe that's a result of the way the Tate has developed up till now, it has been described as five galleries in one.

Well of course the Tate was founded as the National Gallery of British Art, and then had foreign art grafted on to it, so to speak. But I think it is fair to say that you will not be able to make your own connection between Constable and Rothko at Bankside, but there's nothing to stop curators doing that, and devising a display which brings together pictures of different periods, in one or other of the galleries, if we felt it was an interesting thing to be doing. There's no reason, for example, why one couldn't put Hogarth with George Grosz. That's down to the imagination of the curator. What I'm saying is, the visitor won't be able to wander from Constable to Rothko in the same gallery unless we've put them there.

This interview formed the basis of an article published in Artists Newsletter in 1997 (a-n publications)

Part Two

Curators-Collections 2005-2011

The Mausoleum, Dulwich Picture Gallery
Photo: Martin Charles
Courtesy Dulwich Picture Gallery

The Ring of Minos
At The Palace of Knossos

The guide joins the mini-bus on the outskirts of Knossos, picked up at a petrol station. A bullish forty year old he introduces himself briskly to the group with some light hearted banter, gaining confidence in his audience.

Set down at the Palace of Knossos the visitors take advantage of the wash rooms while the guide collects their tickets. The site is crowded with tourists and there are several groups led by specialists. The one in front is steered by a slight woman in a brown and black dress with a star hat and carrying a pale green parasol. She chats in French, German, Greek and English.

The group is directed to steps to the first level of the West Court. The guide points out some possible views to photograph, of the hillside beyond dotted with olive trees. He gives a brief outline of the palace's development, from the first dwelling in 4000 BC, the destruction by fire of the old palace and its reconstitution in 1500 BC, and the eventual closure of Minoan culture by earthquake, volcano eruption and a tsunami that obliterated the settlements on the island of Crete.

The first remains of the palace of Knossos were partially uncovered in 1878 by an amateur archaeologist Minos Kalikairinos, and were thoroughly excavated and archived by Sir Arthur Evans between 1910 to 1913 and 1920 to 1933. The buildings were made of limestone and alabaster quarried from the local hills with the flat roofs supported in three tiers by wooden columns carved from whole cedar trees, whose upended trunks lent a conical shape to the supports, shaped with a ring at the top and base. The structure has been partially restored with concrete beams, coloured to give an illusion of wood grain. The visitors move towards some worn alabaster steps which lead to the Queen's apartment, a shaded cubic space with a door to a bathroom and toilet. The guide explains the Minoan system of irrigation that serviced some 1,400 rooms of the palace. The water was drawn down from the snow capped hills and with rain water was ducted by ceramic pipes laid in two levels: clean water for bathing that drained into a secondary line used to clean waste from the toilets. Each cubicle had a waiting area, with magazines the guide jokes.

The King's apartment adjoined the Queen's, a larger suite with eleven doorways. Here the business of state was conducted. Ambassadors and officials entered certain doors designated for areas of politics, diplomacy, social issues or commerce. The rooms were spacious but not excessive. In accord with the Minoan sense of economy of power they provided what was needed without undue display.

Minoan society was organised in a simple hierarchy; the palace of the King's at Knossos was the largest of five civil palaces in Crete. Below the King and his consuls was an extensive middle class, respected by the ruler for its ability in international trade, which was facilitated by Minoan's great navy. Below the merchant class was a slave class, bound into service to individual families and employed as the labouring stock of the society. There is little evidence of an army, the navy provided a defence of the island, suppressing the threat of piracy or invasion by its overall control of the Mediterranean. Minos was respected by its neighbours for an intelligent use of government. It appears to have been a benign autocracy without expansionist ambitions, happy to operate within the fruitful arena of its island home. Benefiting from the natural resources of a fertile landscape the Minoans exported wine, oil, leathers and artefacts of jewellery and ceramics. Situated 100 miles equally from each continent it traded with Egypt, Greece, Italy, The Phoenicians and Asia. The fortuitous circumstances of a benevolent situation with a reign of enlightened Kings encouraged the flowering over two thousand years of the most sophisticated civilisation; a primary source which informed the emerging Greek culture and its mythology, and acted as a lodestone for the succeeding nation states.

The visitors step down to inspect the Queen's chamber and view a preserved hip bath. They appreciate the cool air of the interior, vented by different levels of passageways and chambers. The Goddess of Fertility and the Sacred Bull dominated Minoan mythology and the palace was decorated throughout by symbolic frescos and on its roofs by votive bull's horns. The guide remarks how early Greek visitors in 4000 BC, unused to the sheer scale and complexity of the first palace, were unable to find their bearings. The network of passageways and chambers painted everywhere with the bull icons bred stories reported home of a minotaur, a half bull-half human creature who occupied the fabled palace, and consumed stray visitors. The fear and drama of this fed into early Greek mythology and had by 1500 BC become the story of the Labyrinth. Tales the Minotaur, Daedalus and Icarus were formed by these first sights of the Palace of Knossos.

The guide is distracted from his monologue by a local visitor who jumps the queue. He engages in a brief but volatile spat of violent invective and gesture. The man trails the group and launches at the guide again furiously, after more screams, swearing and curses he removes his mother, wife and child to complain the palace manager.

"Be my guest" taunts the guide. He then leads the party to view some great ceramic containers preserved from the first phase of the palace. These are two metres high, too bulky to move, and were used to store wine and oil which was vented at the base by a wooden cork or by using a pig's intestine. An eroded circular bowl set in the ground was a wine press, where grapes were trodden and the juice ducted to other containers. In the west wing the group comes on the Magazine, a corridor of cubicles below floor level where vases and other stock was stored under removable floorboards.

On the north aspect is a small amphitheatre which seated four hundred, where spectacles of acrobats and blood sacrifices of animals were staged. A raised platform to the side was reserved for the King and Queen.

The group follows the guide back to the mini-bus for a lunch break, meeting again in the early afternoon in the town centre to explore artefacts of Minos in the municipal museum.

Led by the guide to a somewhat homely arrangement of exhibits the visitors examine minute and exquisite accessories disclosed in excavation: a gold daisy chain necklace, delicate leaf shaped drop earrings and intricate head bands. In another case are rows of small plaster seals. The Minoan state government organised a system of identity checks and passports, allocating a unique picture seal for each individual that signified their occupation. These were archived at the palace and controlled movement and access within the island and elsewhere. Minoans were equally interested to identify their properties, the two storey brick built houses are represented in little faience plaques. A highly sophisticated sense of aesthetic and craft evolved over two thousand years of the Minoan culture. It is particularly evident in the wonderful pottery, where the decoration is bold and dramatic, in white and red patterns on a black ground. Favourite rhythms include spirals and mazes, interlocking images of plants, of sea life; octopuses and dolphins and miniature episodes of mythology, depicting the early gods and goddesses.

In one cabinet is the celebrated Snake Goddess of Fertility; the world famous ikon of a bare breasted woman with a snake in each hand is no more than twelve inches high.

As the guide points out the Minoans did not need to exaggerate scale and were confident to rely on the innate power of their conception. He turns to fire quick questions at his audience, to the children to explain a reason, and compliments a man on his accurate answers. "You have a big imagination" he says. A child points to a newspaper in a vase and an attendant rises defensively as they look inside the vessel. The guide explains how the newsprint was used to secure cracks in the vase and then turns away to chat to some local girls. "Regard the quality of the seals" he encourages close inspection of the moulded discs which carry episodes of dramatic events; a lioness hunting down a bull. On a gold signet ring a goddess leads a winged griffin. A male priest who touches the sacred tree of life. Some small gold ornaments of the double headed axe, a dominant ikon of the second palace period of 1450 BC.

A striking piece figures a Rhyton (sacred offering vessel) made as a bull's head, in black stone incised with spirals and with gilt horns and crystal eyes. Leaf like curls stand for the texture of fur. The guide pauses before a rock crystal vessel from the Palace at Zakros, created from a single piece of clear crystal – a container for votive liquid, from a blood sacrifice. The group cluster around a minute gold pendant of bees with a honeycomb, noting the loose gold orbs held in a little cage. They examine ancient tablets incised with an image script, the mode of

record before the formation of an alphabet. The guide surprises the group with an accounting table from the palace, the first known script to annotate tens and hundreds in units of division. The Phaestos Disc contains symbols in rings of forty five coded images, as yet not completely deciphered. "And what is this?" He indicates a saucer peppered with holes. He hints by pointing out another cabinet which contains teapots and cups with handles. "It's a strainer for mint tea from 2000 BC." Paintings from the palace are exhibited in fragments of original frescos on the upper floor of the museum. Lightly handled in bright colours of pale blue, blood red, chrome, they illustrate festivals and rituals; of male and female acrobats vaulting restrained bulls; pale faced dancers with ornately braided black hair, plaited with ornaments. Partridges nestle in a landscape of waving ferns, humorous pop eyed octopus swirl in the ocean or the leaping dolphins which decorated the Queen's apartment.

And finally he leads the group to the most recent discovery. The fabled Ring of Minos. Discovered in the Queen's chamber at an initial excavation the piece was lost in 1934, and discovered again by as local boy in the past few months glistening in a bush on the hillside. Dismissed by neighbours as a fake it was finally accredited by the museum and purchased for 250,000 euros from the family (who now want more). The hoop of the ring is three fine bands closely set with precious stones and on the sphere of its face are playful gods and goddesses, one who bends the bough of the tree of life, others at ease in an arcadian setting. The left hand female figure is curiously striking with its small head, elongated body, and heavy folded thighs. The image on the face of the ring is so precise and small that it needs photo-enlargements to explain the design. "So maybe I should look for some pieces" says a visitor. "Sure, there is

The Ring of Minos, Minoan, Circa 1900 BC
Archaeological Museum of Heraklion.

still a lot to find here" says the guide, "but you can't take them out of the country" "Why, they'd cut my hand off?" "No they're not Arabs, the museum will buy them, they'll pay well for them." Replies the guide.

The group inspects some human bones in an open sarcophagus. "Notice the position" says the guide. "it is folded like a foetus. At the end they returned the body to its birth." With this reflection the tour ends and the visitors return to the waiting mini-bus for transport back to their hotels.

Excavation of the Palace of Knossos

Knossos emerged from a neolithic settlement on Crete from 5700 to 2800 BC. The first palace of the Kings was constructed on a low plateau (Kefala) inland from the valleys of Herakleion and Karteros. It was constructed from limestone quarried from the surrounding hills. The area was abundant in olive groves, and benefited from the source of the Karratos river and Therron tributary which flowed down to the port of Knossos. In earlier times the hills were covered with forests of cypress and oak which were utilised in the palace's construction.

Destroyed by natural disaster, fire and earthquake, the ancient palace of Knossos remained concealed until 1878 when a Herakleion businessman and amateur archaeologist Minos Kalikairinos unearthed part of the store rooms on the West aspect of the palace. He donated the large storage jars (pithoi) to several major museums, and otherwise retained discoveries in his private collection, which was destroyed in a social insurgence of 1898. Beyond that Turkish owners of the land resisted offers from interested archaeologists until Sir Arthur Evans purchased the site in 1900. With permission of the Cretan State he began a major excavation from 1900-02, funded by his personal resources. He was assisted by leading specialists Mackenzie, Hogarth, Wace, Forsdyke, Pendlebury, Paynes and Hutchison. Evans achieved a major reconstitution of the palace, working on site to 1912, and resuming the project from 1922 to 1931, when the Southern Royal Tomb was discovered.

He published his findings in six volumes entitled The Palace of Minos at Knossos, which became a keystone for subsequent archaeological projects in Crete. Other aspects of the palace were revealed after the Second World War by the Minoan scholar S.Hood, who uncovered of a number of tombs. Work is presently at a standstill due to the massive Greek investment in staging the last Olympic Games, but will eventually be resumed. The concerns now are for consolidation of the fragile palace structure which is suffering from an incessant and formidable tourist flow to the site.

Layout of the Palace of Knossos

The West Court leading to three
processional ways.
The Western Magazines (Storage compartments
with large vases – pithoi).
The Throne Room Complex including
The Lustral Basin .
Complex of the Central Shrine
The Central Court
The Royal Apartments (Megarons) including
The Hall of the Double Axes,
And the site of Rhia's Temple .
The King's Megaron and The Queen's Megaron.
A workshop area for potters and stonemasons.

The Court of the Stone Spout .
The Great East Hall including the Corridor
of the Draught Board .
The Customs House .
The complex of
the Northern Entrance and the Northwest area.
The Theatre including underground rooms
The Old Palace was destroyed c.1700 BC.
The New Palace was overbuilt and itself
destroyed three times from 1600-1500 BC.

Phases of Minoan Civilisation
The timeline of the Minoan Palaces divides as the Pre-Palatial
period (2800-1900 BC), The Old Palace Period (1900-1700 BC);
The New Palace Period (1700-1400 BC) and the Post Palatial
Period (1400-1100 BC). Beyond the Bronze Age of 2800-1100
BC comes the Iron Age (1100-67 BC). These included a num-
ber of phases making Minoan civilization: the Sub-Minoan
and Early Geometric Period (1100-900 BC); The Geometric
Period (900-750 BC); Early Archaic (650-500 BC); Classical
(500-323 BC) and Hellenstro Period (323-67 BC).

The Myths of Knossos
Ancient Greek myths draw their source from the legends
of Minos King of Knossos. Minos was born son of Zeus
and Europa, a Phoenician nymph. Minos was born with
his brothers Rhadamanthys and Sarpedon in the region
of Gortyn on Crete. Abandoned by Zeus Europa married
Asterius, King of Crete, who adopted her sons. Minos
married Pasiphaë, daughter of Helios the Sun God, bear-
ing four sons and four daughters: Catreus, Xenodike,
Ariadne, Androgenus, Glaucus, Deucalion, Phaedra and
Accalis. The god Poseidon instills love in Pasiphaë for
the great White Bull which sprang from the sea. She
conjoins with the bull and from their union comes the
half bull-half human Minotaur (Asterius) who is then
imprisoned by Minos in the Labyrinth, created by the
master craftsman of Athens Daedalus. Ariadne assists
the hero Theseus to enter the Labyrinth where he slays
the Minotaur. Theseus, complying with the will of the
gods abandons Ariadne on the Isle of Naxos, leaving her
to Dionysius. From their union are born Stephylos,
Theus and Oenopion.

Pithoi 2000 BC at The Palace of Knossos
Cv/VAR Archive

References:
Minoan Crete Andonis Vasilikis
Knossos Andonis Vasilikis
(Both published by Adam Editions, Athens)

The Ring of Minos N.P.James ©
First published in 2005

Curator's Progress

Ian A.C. Dejardin,
Director of Dulwich Picture Gallery,
interviewed in February 2010

Cv/VAR We're going to discuss what it's like to lead a major institution of art. First of all, in your own career path to this position, how did you begin?

ID It's peculiar, my career. Obviously I started out with my degree, which was in art history; I was going to do a postgraduate, a Phd, but I dropped out of that, it wasn't working. Oddly enough thereafter, I started in crafts. I set up my own business designing and making knitwear, believe it or not. I thought I've got the cottage industry, I want the cottage as well. I moved to the Lake District and had an absolutely blissful time in my twenties; living and pottering about in the Lakes and just about managing to survive. I was a member of the Guild of Lakeland Craftsmen, I put on minor exhibitions of my work, it was useful experience. When I decided to grow up, basically, and thought the money would be nice, I retrained. I went to Manchester and did a postgraduate diploma in art gallery studies there. The point about this preamble is that, funnily enough, in those days there were only about seventeen days on that course. I got on because, though I did have a First Class Honours Degree in art history, but then so did lots of other people, and I got on because I had experience of running my own business and mounting exhibitions of my own work.

The seed bed was the knitting?
That's right. It led to where I am today so I always give it full credit. Once I'd got my diploma I was very lucky, because I was already in my thirties, and was clearly seen as a more mature junior person, I got a wonderful job straight away; I was very briefly at English Heritage. I moved on to The Royal Academy very quickly as curatorial assistant, and it was a tremendous learning curve. I had two and a half years at The Royal Academy where I did everything in the curatorial department. When I left there I was replaced by three people and realised I'd been overworked. I enjoyed it hugely and I learnt everything. I was working in the photographic department, I was working as a library assistant; looking after the permanent collection, cataloguing the works in plaster. It was great and then I went back to English Heritage as senior curator of paintings. Again I think I was lucky; I looked the part, I was thirty four and had specialised in paintings at university.

At English Heritage what area were you looking after, the whole span of the UK?
No it was the London Region and that was the only part I was interested in. When I left English Heritage after the eight month contract at the very beginning of my career, I looked over my shoulder and hoped if ever Kenwood House comes up, let me know, and they did. That was part of my brief. So I was senior curator for the paintings at London's historic houses. That included Kenwood House, Ranger's House, Chiswick

House, Marble Hill; I was curator for all of them and I had a lovely time.

English Heritage being what it was they restructured every two years. They would bring in McKinsey and do a management report and decide we were staffed all wrong. Fortunately I was one of the few that sailed serenely through this, as there was no-one else with real expertise in paintings. And although, as far as I was concerned I was doing the same job, my job description got more and more grand over the seven years I was there. I ended up as head of the historic team and senior curator.

So this was a very good track record in management, what about aspects of conservation?

I learned about conservation very early on at The Royal Academy, because effectively I was running the conservation programme. I was an art historian by my university training, but I had to learn the practical aspects, pretty well on the hoof. The diploma that I got in Art Gallery Studies, was excellent but it was only a course of nine months or so. You got a pretty good grounding in the basics of what conservation required, but at The Royal Academy I was working with some very good conservators, who were incredibly experienced; so I learned very quickly, a reason I was employed.

Right in the beginning I was reporting to Mary Anne Stevens, the RA librarian, who was a great boss and a good person to respond to. When I went on to English Heritage I was in charge of the picture conservation programme there. At that date the AMSEE conservation studio was based in the stable block at Kenwood,

and I was lucky to work with some very good conservators there. I became curator here at Dulwich Picture Gallery after that, in 1998.

I had done everything in a rather condensed way to that point. Funnily enough, when I was interviewed for this job it was assumed I was stepping down, my job description at English Heritage sounded so grand at this stage. But actually what I wanted was a collection, a single collection that I could identify with and work very closely with. At English Heritage I had very quickly become more of a manager. For a while I was working in the centre at Oxford Street, and my assistant curators, of whom I had several, were doing all the interesting stuff.

So you found yourself floating into management?

Absolutely, which I actually enjoyed but at that date I really wanted to focus on a collection and I thought it was the right move to make at that point. I also knew it was the right moment to come to Dulwich. The job had come up two and a half years before and I hadn't gone for it, because the circumstances were very different then. When they advertised again they had announced the building project and I was interested.

What state was the gallery in when you arrived?

It was charming and tatty, but the gallery was already on the up, with exhibitions underway. I'm only the third director here. The first was Giles Waterfield and he had taken on a gallery which was funded by a school, it was part of Dulwich College and funded by an

Interior View
Dulwich Picture Gallery

inadequate stipend.

No government support, no arts council support, or local authority funding?

No, we were funded by the school. Giles did miracles in the twenty-odd years he worked here. He really put it on the map and established education as a priority here. When I arrived Desmond Shaw Taylor had taken over two years before. Desmond is an academic, he's now Surveyor of the Queen's Pictures. Dulwich Picture Gallery became an independent trust in 1994, with no government funding; we have an endowment that brings in about a quarter of what we need. Another quarter comes from admissions-revenue and sales in the shop. I have to raise about half of what we need to operate, that's about £1.5 million a year, in order to do everything we do; education, collection management, exhibitions. There's nothing in the budget to cover them.

You took over the gallery as curator and were then appointed director.

Seven years later. In those days the post of curator looked after exhibitions as well, as it does again now, but there was a hiatus. When I was at Kenwood I was a kind of one man band doing the exhibitions there.

What was the state of the gallery when you came here?

In 1998 it was a moment of change. They were just building up to the refurbishment of 1999, to the new extension and gallery refurbishment, so again my experience of hanging, of looking after collections, was one of the reasons I was employed. At that point fifty of our greatest paintings went off to Japan and toured, another fifty went to Spain. The two groups came together in a couple of venues in the States. I managed all of that. I think I must be the only curator in its two hundred year history who has had to re-hang the whole gallery from scratch.

It's a great collection, is most of it on show?

No, two thirds of it is in store and this is a sore point with me. We are the oldest purpose built art gallery in England, from our foundation in 1811, but the old college was founded in Jacobean times with a bequest of paintings; so there have actually been paintings on this site for four hundred years. Those early collections are still here; they're not great

Ian A.C.Dejardin,
Director, Dulwich Picture Gallery

names, but they are historically fascinating. Because I am an exhibitions person by nature and an interpretation person, I long to get them out and show people, but there just isn't room.

So apart from the special exhibitions, such as the present one of Paul Nash, you can't revolve what is hanging on the wall.

No, it's an interesting problem to have. The fact of the matter is that exhibitions are life blood for institutions. We hold three major exhibitions a year and that's what brings, I would say, ninety percent of the visitors. They also have to stop and go through the gallery, they see that as well. But it is a problem that a lot of museums have. I cannot justify using all of the galleries for the permanent collection. I keep that particular suite of rooms for exhibitions, they are continuous now. If I had a magic wand and could conjure up a new wing on the side of the building, the permanent collection could fill the Soane Gallery, and that would be ideal.

You mentioned touring some pictures. What scope is there in international terms, and what interest is there from abroad in what you're holding?

It varies, and we've just had another experience which has not been quite so smooth. Our Dutch Italianate paintings, forty of them are hung in a traditional 'historic' hang at Dulwich, so they fill a room from floor to ceiling very densely. We needed the room for other displays last year and decided to send them touring, because I'd rather they were touring than in store. So with an American exhibition broker we took them to four exhibition venues in the States. Practically as soon as they were out of the door the world's economy crashed, and I think, to be honest, that may be the last time we do it.

What was the implication of that?

Well one of the museums has gone bankrupt.

Oh my God.

We've got them back, you'll be delighted to know.

Might not have done.

The museum went bankrupt after our show had left them, thank goodness, and they paid. So there was a risk which we hadn't anticipated; nobody had anticipated the world's economy crashing. It has seriously revealed the dangers of that kind of touring show. In normal times, in boom times I think it's a good thing to do, because works of art are for everybody, they shouldn't just sit still. That's also very important to us because we depend on loans for our exhibitions, so we have to be generous with our works.

What suggested the Paul Nash exhibition, was it a family collection, did it surface as a topic of historical interest in modern British art?

I think in series, I always do, and I think it's a sensible thing in exhibition programming, to have a related series of exhibitions. David Fraser Jenkins came to me and Desmond Shaw Taylor, when he was director, way back in 2001 or '02; at that point David was the senior curator of British art at Tate Britain. I think he felt it wasn't Tate policy at that point to show exhibitions of the great British modernists, so David thought there was a gap in the market. He came with a list of artists' names and asked if Dulwich would be interested in any of these as the subject of an exhibition. Coincidentally Desmond and I were both looking around at that moment, at ways of expanding the exhibition programme.

Both of us were fans of 20th century British modernism, so we said, let's look into it. As a result of that meeting David co-curated with Frances Spalding, his first show here in 2003, which was 'John Piper in the 1930s'. That was a beautiful show and it was a pleasure working with David; he's a very experienced curator. Working through David's list, I then co-curated Henry Moore here in 2004. It was a great show, based on the collections of the Sainsbury Centre, which was closed for refurbishment. So Robert and Lisa Sainsbury's collection was the core of that exhibition, but much expanded. We then did Graham Sutherland. Now no-one has thought about Graham Sutherland since he died, and that was the

first exhibition that had been given to him since then. Paul Nash was the obvious next one. We had wanted to do Paul Nash first of all, but the Tate were doing a Liverpool show at that point.

Where are the works by Paul Nash drawn from?

All over. A lot of private collections. David had done such a lot of research into the field. For this exhibition in particular he was really interested in identifying paintings that were known about only through photographs, that had disappeared. This was very much the case with Piper as well. Many of those paintings by Piper, particularly from the 1930s, had gone to ground in private collections. They were often sold to friends of the artist or just private buyers. They were owned by grandchildren who perhaps didn't realise what they had, and the same is true of Nash. David set out to identify as many of those as he could. So there are about a dozen paintings from private collection that haven't been seen for an awful long time. Of course the great works from the Government Art Collection and the Tate are in there as well. First of all we had to establish that the major institutional owners of Nash, like the Tate and the Imperial War Museum, would lend.

Can we touch on your coordination of your exhibition programming with other galleries? A programme after all is organised all over and in particular. So do you meet, do you convey to each other your secret dreams?

Not as much as it would be helpful to do.

How good is the state of negotiation between institutions?

Pretty good. The only problem is, exhibition programming by its general nature tends to be rather secretive; in that you don't want everyone to know what you're planning.

But you don't want any nasty clashes that cause deep embarrassment.

Exactly, the Paul Nash was an example of that, where we even started work on a show in 2002; then found the Tate was doing a big show. Of course there was no competition, we simply had to gracefully withdraw. That occasionally happens but not very often. It is interesting that the world is full of institutions, from our size up to the giants, who are all working away, producing exhibition programmes. There ought to be a lot more communication than there is, because collaboration is a very good way of doing it. This show, Paul Nash, interestingly is unique to us.

Exhibitions fall into different camps really, and we do all of them. Paul Nash, unique to us, no collaborator. More often than not we will find a collaborator; there are two main ways of doing it: either you generate the show, send it off to the collaborator and they pay a fee that covers administration, and buy catalogues on sale or return. Or, more frequently, you set up a contractual relationship, in which the collaboration is divided neatly down the middle. You estimate what the budget is going to be for the entire tour, say for two or three venues maximum, and divide it up accordingly. Transport is divided, the catalogue cost is divided in two, curatorial costs in two; the institution pays for its own marketing, its own location and specific expenses.

Is private or corporate sponsorship harder to find now?

It's coming out of the woods now. Last year was difficult, we cancelled one show but, I don't like quoting that as an example of credit crunch planning. We had a gap in the programme which was caused by the need to postpone a show for other reasons. I tried to find a replacement in a short time, which was difficult; you really need a year, or year and a half before running an exhibition, minimum. I had six months. I had the exhibition, which was a big one of Hiroshige prints from Rome, which would have been gorgeous and was a huge hit there, but, in those circumstances the trustees were not prepared to proceed unless we had demonstrated that we were going to get the money. We had one major sponsor lined up, the discussions were very productive, very positive looking, and then at the last minute they just decided, no.

And at that moment we decided, no we couldn't go on, couldn't risk it, so we did another show instead, based on our own collection, incidentally it was a great success. Dulwich is rather special, it doesn't really relate to other institutions; we have no government funding, no local council funding, all of our activities depend on fund raising, it's always been like that. The credit crunch and economic collapse did affect us, but it didn't affect the way we run, because we already run on a shoestring.

We are prepared to turn on a sixpence. So if an exhibition is cancelled, I can move very quickly to replace it or to change track. There's no question of ticking boxes, which is one of the burdens of being a national. We have to meet the same standards as all other institutions, but we can go our own way.

Seed Structures

The work of the Contemporary Art Society.

Interview with Lucy Byatt,
Head of National Programme CAS

Cv/VAR How did you come to work for The Contemporary Art Society?
LB I was director of an organisation called Spike Island in Bristol, and before that I worked in Glasgow; I ran a commissioning organisation there for ten years. I took the job as director of Spike and we went through a capital development programme, restructuring the nature of that organisation. What was important about that; it wasn't just rebuilding, it was really thinking through how one develops a culture around a facility. How do you use that space, what is the agency that creates a community of interest around an institution of that sort? Not one with a strong curator at the gate but much more an amalgam of voices that are actually dictating the public programme. That seemed to be a suitable philosophy to come out of what had been an artist run organisation in the 1970s. I was there for six or seven years and a good friend of mine said to me, "Lucy, you've become so local." This was true for how I was feeling, and I did want a job with a national perspective.
You then moved to work for The Contemporary Art Society.
This job at CAS emerged and it was a very interesting one. It was at a time when the organisation entering a new generative period with a new director. I joined as part of the programming side

of it. One is working here in a very different silo to the culture to Spike Island, but in a sense it's quite similar, in that one has to have a very broad perspective and be a catalytic agent, if you like, across a broad membership of institutions that have a relationship to the Contemporary Art Society and its collections. They are to an extent stakeholders of the Society.
You are working with member museums but there's a definition within that?
What the organisation was set up to do in 1910 and still does in 2010; it's renewed its vows if you like, it acquires and gifts contemporary art, art of the time, to public collections across the country. It also has a role to educate the public and more generally its members about contemporary art. The Society was first set up as a group of patrons, who felt that there was a need for a strong voice to find a way for the new art to find a way into the national collections. That's still what we do today. We work with artists who are showing quite broadly, and internationally, within the art gallery environment, but may not yet be represented in public collections.
This is interesting, because I had assumed the museums decide their own purchases. What you're saying is there's a kind of bridge building going on.
Originally the Contemporary Art Society was called *The Distribution Scheme*, and they would gather people together they thought were the great, the good and interesting; and they would buy works for an exhibition. Museum curators would come along and decide which was their first, second and third choice.

There were debates and differences of opinion and some curators would never get the work they wanted. Then later on, through the '90s, there was The Special Collections Scheme, which was a lottery funded project at £3 million. This was a building-based capital project set up to work with fifteen museums to buy works. This was a big change, certainly it can be seen now that the curators who were involved became much more confident and active about how to work with their collections. The scheme created a network; to research, to do studio visits, national trips and so on.

The curator has certainly emerged as an important factor in the general cultural process.

In the past fifteen years we've seen a burgeoning of curatorial courses and, if you like, there's a new profession. But that hasn't necessarily impacted the museums yet. The old definition of the curator was somebody who'd come out of an art historical background and who cared for the collection. They engaged the audiences in a highly educational experience. I think there is a different definition for the role of the curator within contemporary art: active, entrepreneurial, a maker and breaker of artists, if you like. Somebody who brings new artists to the fore, who haven't quite hit the museum sector.

We're still working with curators who have been with the same collections for a very long time, and they think about exhibitions in relation to that responsibility; to educate through an art historical trajectory. But things are changing and it is a time to be thinking about how these new ideas of curators are going to have an effect on the museums in the next ten or fifteen years. I also think that collections are pregnant with possibilities for curators who haven't yet thought of the placement of new work.

With regard to your work as Head of National Programme at CAS, what does that cover?

Referring to the work of distribution, I run the new acquisitions scheme. This year we have a three stranded programme. One strand is where we work with museums to buy works they think best fit their acquisition policy. We do a lot of research together, it's intensive, and at the end of the process we buy a work together. Last year we worked with nine museums, this year it's fifteen. Sometimes we introduce a museum to new artists. They don't necessarily purchase but do an exhibition, so there are lots of outcomes from the research period.

Another strand is the national network; a membership programme for curators, predominantly those who are working with collections. We developed a programme of one or two events a month that curators come to. This focuses on developing issues; around the collection, working with artists, developing online resources. It can be skills orientated or much more theoretical.

The national network is very much a forum for curators to be thinking about the cultural value of collections; how they can be used and evolved. I suppose the central aim of that is to be investing slowly, in a grass roots way, in generating new curators of the future.

Turning to the other side of CAS, its member collectors.

Out of the origins of early supporters who gathered in 1910 to establish the organisation, has come over the years, various attitudes towards how one builds a body of patrons, and probably the number of members is larger than it's ever been. We sometimes have conversations about whether they share the aims of the charity, which is to work with public collections. One of the things we do is to girder the support of private collectors; people who have an interest and enthusiasm, an expertise in contemporary art. There is a programme that introduces those people to the collections, who pay to join it.

We engage them with how they may be able to help work with the public sector. So, for instance, we have an annual award, funded by one of our patrons, for a museum. I just had a conversation with somebody who wants to fund a five year project with five museums, to generate a new collection of sculptureyear project with five museums, to generate a new collection of sculpture. We work with member collectors to translate what their interests and fascinations are to the public sector. We can make that transferral.

Where do private galleries fit in with this?

Private galleries are enormously important because they represent the artists we buy. It's rare that we go directly to the artists to purchase their work, but often we go through the galleries.

The galleries are aware they want their artists' work to be in public collections. Increasingly we also have a policy where we ask the museums who purchase to show that work in the first year or so of the work entering the collection. So if asked, do we affect the public programme of those institutions? Yes we are beginning to. One hopes that, by buying with those institutions, those are works the curators are really excited by anyway. So, for instance, in the coming year the New Walk Gallery Leicester will be showing a work by Rosalind Nashashibi that we've just purchased. Aberdeen Art Gallery will be showing a new work by Emily Wardill. Marcus Coates work will be shown at the Walker Art Gallery in Liverpool.

How does the CAS interface with other bodies: the RSA, the Art Fund, the Arts Council, how do you all work together?

The Art Fund and the CAS come out of a very similar history, and were invented at a similar time, in similar contexts. One was about preserving historic works of art, treasures, and the other was about contemporary art. There is a lot of work to be done with museums so the more bodies that are working in a complementary way, a collegiate way, the better. CAS has a member structure unlike any other, its sixty three member organisations are its core. The really amazing idea was the was the invention of a network across the whole of the United Kingdom, that has sustained over a hundred years. That is absolutely the gem of what CAS is.

What is interesting is the very individual identities of regional museums.

They are extraordinarily different, like apples and pears. Small and large, and attitudinally they are very different from one another. They have very different ambitions and management structures.

Saved for the Future

*Interview with Dr Stephen Deuchar,
Director, The Art Fund*

Cv/VAR First of all, a brief history of the Art Fund ?

SD It was formed in 1903 by a group what we might call today 'do gooders' – members of high society, art professionals and so on - who were worried about the potential and indeed the actual drain away from Britain of great works of art to foreign collectors. The group decided to lead by example, putting money into a fund which would be available for museums to help them purchase works of art that might otherwise go abroad.

From that small beginning - the first executive committee comprised eighteen individuals - we have moved to a membership of eighty thousand today. With the resources that those members give us we continue to provide funds either to stop works of art going abroad, or simply to help museums make acquisitions. So our core purpose remains pretty much the same - to support museums in acquiring great works of art for the benefit of the wider public. Public benefit drives us and is the reason for our existence.

You have been involved in campaigns in recent years, which have included saving Turner's great watercolour 'Blue Rigi' from export?

Yes, the 'Blue Rigi' campaign took place when I was director of Tate Britain, and that was the challenge of raising some £5 million to save this exceptional watercolour from export. We approached the Art Fund to run a public campaign for us, which they did, and it produced a huge response. And with the very strong additional support of the National Heritage Memorial Fund, the full sum was raised within about eight weeks of the campaign's launch.

Can we go into what happens to a work of art? Often a work is on extended loan to a museum and then, for whatever reason, the owner decides to dispose of the work. Is there an opportunity for negotiation in this process?

The 'Blue Rigi' was sold at auction to an overseas buyer, so the price was set by that sale. The Export Review Committee put a bar on its export, and we at the Tate were given a period of time to match that sum, and so the vendor received exactly the same amount of money in the end as he would have done if the sale had gone ahead to the original buyer. So in such instances there isn't any real negotiation about the sum of money involved.

In the case of a work of art that's been on loan to a museum for a long time, as with Titian's Diana and Actaeon at the National Gallery of Scotland, a negotiation over price can of course take place between buyer and seller, informed by valuations, assessments of the market, the pecuniary needs of the vendor and so on. The sum of money in that instance was agreed at £50 million.

These are extraordinary sums of money.

They are, though some might say that if the works went to public auction the price would be even higher.

So a special group of people can be approached to save a work, but then, in the campaign, you throw it open to the public and other interventions, artists join in; I'm thinking here of Lucian Freud's appearance to speak for Titian's Diana and Actaeon. Can you tell how alive the public is to the importance of these works for the country?

There's definitely a distinction to be drawn between works of art that are perceived to be under threat, in danger of slipping away, and works of art that are simply being acquired because museums want them.

Art Fund members are certainly very susceptible, if that's the right word, to an appeal where there's a real danger that something important will disappear from these shores if they don't intervene. When it's a question of coming up with a large sum of money just to fund a normal purchase, you have to work a little bit harder to put the argument across: why does a museum need 'yet another' portrait by Sir Thomas Lawrence, say.

Works under threat are an easier proposition from a campaigning point of view. We've recently concluded our campaign to raise £3.3 million to save the Staffordshire Hoard, that extraordinary group of Anglo Saxon treasures - some 1,600 individual items.

We quite rightly talked about 'saving' the Staffordshire Hoard, but it wasn't yet subject to an export-stop, indeed it hadn't yet come onto the open market. We merely knew that if the money wasn't raised the works could have been dispersed, or sold as a group abroad. So what we were doing in that instance was pre-empting those possibilities, by acting to stop the work going up for open sale.

How do you evaluate a discovery? Is your response instant and intuitive?

I would have to say no. Our response can be fast but it's always carefully considered. Of course, as individuals we have an instinct about things and a sense of whether something should be supported or not. The Trustees of the Art Fund consider every application for a sum of money and they look at it from all angles. They view the work at first hand, solicit whatever additional opinions they need, but make their decision based on the evidence brought before them. These are very careful, rational decisions.

As it happens, in the case of the Staffordshire Hoard, there was a very quick, strong, almost overwhelming sense this was a very important body of work that must be saved and the Art Fund was in a position to help; so it wasn't a very difficult decision to make.

I do think that the Fund's Trustees would guard quite jealously its reputation as a body which only supports works of art that are truly significant. And they would avoid the spontaneous, instinctive decision in favour of a carefully considered one, where they could.

And the Staffordshire Hoard will be housed in a particular place and made available to the public?

Yes, works purchased with the Art Fund only ever end up in the public domain. In this instance the two designated museums are the Stoke Potteries Museum and the Birmingham Museum and Art Gallery. Between them they will house the Hoard and research will be undertaken under their auspices. Any exhibition tours will be undertaken under their organisation. They will be the owners.

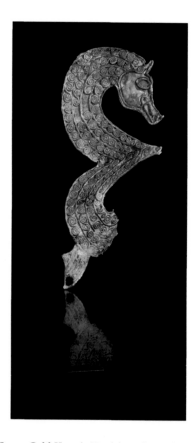

Anglo-Saxon Gold Horse's Head from the Staffordshire Hoard. The Art Fund led the £3.3million campaign to save the Staffordshire Hoard for the Birmingham Museums and Art Gallery and the Potteries Museum and Art Gallery in Stoke-on-Trent.
© Staffordshirehoard.org.uk and Birmingham Museum and Art Gallery. Curtesy of the Art Fund

This isn't the only work of the Art Fund, dealing with major finds and works, because there are numerous front that the Fund is working on; amounts of work in all historical categories. Do galleries and museums approach the Art Fund for, say a piece of porcelain, or for a particular fairly obscure work? Is there a criteria that is applied.

We do indeed give grants and pursue activities on a variety of fronts, but it's not actually that complicated. At the heart of our charitable activities is our main grants programme. There is a special category of small grants up to £5,000, which our Trustees deal with quite swiftly by email. Any museum that wants to acquire something and can put up a strong case for acquisition can apply, and our Trustees can decide quickly to offer support. If it's an auction and they need a very fast decision we can comply. But the main body of applications come to the Trustee meetings which take place every two months. At a typical meeting we might consider between fifteen and thirty applications, which can range in value from a few thousand to a few hundred thousand or more. We give away about £5million pounds a year in total.

The Art Fund receives grants?

The principal grant is money from our members, by subscription, which produces an income of two to three million pounds a year. In addition we have some Trusts and Foundations which lend support either on an ongoing basis or in response to specific appeals. We received several large donations for the Staffordshire Hoard, that were channelled through to us in the general campaign. We have a small amount of capital, nothing very significant by charity standards, but that creates some additional income as well.

Lottery funding?

We're in receipt of no public money at all. We're entirely privately funded. It's an independent charity.

Is that The Art Fund's preference?

It is the preference of the Trustees, because it gives us complete independence. We're not subject to the rules of Government funding which apply to taxpayers' money. So we're able to be quite flexible and responsive which suits us well.

But we do work in collaboration with public funding sources in some instances.

I was thinking of the major campaigns, whether the Lottery might intervene to help?

Well indeed. Take the Staffordshire Hoard, for example, where the National Heritage Memorial Fund came in with a grant of £1.2 million, which we effectively bid for on the basis of what we ourselves had contributed and raised. But we think there is an important distinction to be drawn between acting in collaboration with public funding and actually being a conduit for tax payers' money which, the Trustees might argue, could constrain their freedom and effectiveness.

I interviewed Steve McQueen about 'Queen and Country' and it suggested to me that you are open to artists' projects. He was an Official War Artist and you have an active campaign for his memorial stamps.

Yes we helped the Imperial War Museum to acquire his work 'Queen and Country' – in fact we paid for it outright - so that was a standard Art Fund grant. As a result of that grant, we learned that Steve was very keen to take forward the idea of the stamps becoming a reality and asked us to support his campaign to make this happen, which we were happy to do. Usually our campaigns would not be of this kind; they would be for museum sector issues - famously, for example, for free admission. And when the NHMF funding was briefly threatened with a major cut by the DCMS earlier this year we worked with other institutions to argue against it. Again, being independent of Government gives us the ability to campaign as we see fit.

Another really interesting project is Artist Rooms, from Anthony d'Offay's collection. What involvement did The Art Fund have in enabling that?

To start with, we gave £1 million to help acquire the work.

It's an extraordinary collection.

It is an exceptionally important collection. We gave grants to the Tate and the National Galleries of Scotland - one of many sources of funding, but for us a million pounds was a huge commitment. And having made that commitment we decided we would also like to support the tour of Artist Rooms across the country. I think this is a remarkable, even ground breaking project; taking works of very high quality into communities that might rarely get the opportunity to see works of real importance right on their doorstep. So we effectively worked like an exhibition sponsor to enable that process to unfold.

That must have had a very enlivening effect on the venues where the Rooms turned up?

I think so, yes, it was a brilliant idea that had and continues to have a really significant public impact.

How does the Art Fund interface with other arts organisations; member societies etc?

Well we overlap to some extent with certain organisations, for example the Contemporary Art Society, or the National Heritage Memorial Fund, each in a very different way. Despite our different constitutions we are each giving money out to enable institutions to buy works of art, so noteworthy

Six Haute Couture Dresses by Madeleine Vionnet were purchased in 2009 by three museums: the Bowes Museum, Barnard Castle; Fashion Museum, Bath and the V&A, London with Art Fund assistance. Photo © V&A Images . Courtesy The Art Fund

You came to the Art Fund in January 2010. You had a feel for it because you worked with it from Tate Britain; can you sum up what you think its strength and purpose is?

I do think the Art Fund is quite a remarkable organisation. To be directly involved, as we are, in the purchase of some eighty percent of museum acquisitions above the level of one hundred thousand pounds, across the country, year in, year out, is extraordinary. For such a crucial national role to be be performed by an independent charity, supported by ordinary members of the public, seems to me to be pretty noteworthy I still seems to me to be pretty noteworthy. I still find myself in awe of the speed and generosity and the effectiveness of the Trustees and their work. I do think the Art Fund is a vital part of the art scene, all the more so these days with government funding drying up or under threat on all fronts. To have a body to help museums carry on acquiring when times are very difficult, and to support curators, to stop important works from slipping from their grasp – well, I think that really matters.

it's very important we have a good strong relationship with each other. I want the Art Fund to be very open, very collaborative, and to suppress any sense of competition. We need to make sure that the end game, which is public benefit, is properly served.

Well particularly as, art being what it is, a fickle animal, produces volatile feelings and reactions.

Indeed it does, but provided we keep our eye on our overall purposes, serving the public interest and helping works of art come into the public domain, all will be well.

The Gathering

*Interview with Jill Constantine
recorded at ACE Depot in May 2010*

Cv/VAR You're Senior Curator of the Arts Council Collection. How long have you been here?
JC I've worked with the collection about thirty years, but not always in this capacity.
So you know it pretty well?
I think I know it better than most, probably more than anybody now.
What were the beginnings of the Arts Council Collection?
It was post-war, CEMA, (Council for the Encouragement of Music and the Arts, which existed during the last war), were given a group of paintings by The Pilgrim Trust. In 1946, when the Arts Council was formed, these paintings were given to what was then, the Arts Council of Great Britain and that's when the Collection began. The aim, at the time, was to make small touring exhibitions in order to introduce the general public to contemporary visual art.
I've got an image here of a Henry Moore figure drawing, 1937, so this would have been bringing together works from the 1930s onwards? I'm thinking about the time frame for contemporary art.
I think our collecting is about looking at what is happening at the time in British art. As the Collection has been in existence for nearly sixty five years we describe our holdings as modern and contemporary. It's a constant subject for discussion, where modern art ends and contemporary art begins. The Moore drawing, you mention, may have been

acquired by Sir Kenneth Clark as part of a group of work, which included some bronze maquettes, which he bought directly from the artist for the Collection in 1948. This group is an example of where we bought historically, but most of the collection dates from post 1946. We do have five works by Sickert in our collection, but that is unusual and probably reflects a period when the acquisition policy was possibly less structured than in later times. It's not clear what the policy was at the time, apart from collecting the best of British modern art.
So that would have been a specialist committee, and you mentioned Kenneth Clark.
Yes, some very distinguished people have advised on acquisitions. As well as Sir Kenneth Clark, David Sylvester and Brian Robertson, sat on what was called the Arts Panel which had a general advisory role. Later, it became a more formalised process. In the 1970s a proper acquisitions committee was established and people were invited to be on that committee. The process has always been to have a certain number of external advisers to work with the internal advisers.
So jumping forward to now, how is an acquisitions committee composed?
It usually includes a critic, an artist, and an independent curator. The acquisitions committee is chaired by the Head of the Collection. The other permanent members are, the Director of the Hayward Gallery, a representative from Arts Council England, and myself. The reason for having outside advisers is to bring a new perspective into the discussions. They will sit on the committee for two years and then it

changes. People put forward names and we discuss who may bring a fresh view. They aren't necessarily given a formal brief, in the sense of telling them what to buy but they must be well acquainted with contemporary art practice. For example, this year there was a desire amongst the new members of the committee to look at contemporary photography. There is a great deal of research involved. Everyone visits as many exhibitions as they can, whether public or commercial galleries.

Artists don't submit their work directly, I presume?

Artists can, there is still open submission. They can send in proposals which we will look at. If there's something we feel we would like to see we will follow that up and make studio visits to an artist or if that is difficult they can bring their work in for us to see.

Across the country?

Yes, anybody living in the UK, or even British artists living abroad if their work is relevant to current British art practice then, yes. We might have to draw the line on a studio visit, if someone has a studio abroad, because of sheer cost.

As I came in we looked at a work by George Shaw. How did that process of purchase evolve?

By seeing shows and through contact with other collections; for example Southampton Art Gallery own a very fine work by him. You become aware of good work and what should be in the Arts Council Collection. As it's a loan collection, you are always aware of the work people will be interested in and want to borrow. We'd seen his work last year in a show at his

dealers in the East End. We were struck by it but felt we wanted to see further work, so we didn't buy at the time. In the end, just a few weeks ago the Committee settled on this particular painting from that original show.

It's a fine work. This leads me on to your capacity to purchase works. The art market, as we know, is wildly volatile and variable. How do you feel you're positioned in this particular arena?

Well, like every public collection we'd like more money for acquisitions. However, we are better funded than some other collections.

Do you accept donations?

We do get donated works. For example, Charles Saatchi gave us two gifts, very generous ones, in 1998 and 2002. Individual artists have also donated work including Bridget Riley and Wolfgang Tillmans in 2009. We also seek funding from The Art Fund and have been successful on a number of occasions, they've been very helpful. Our acquisitions budget is about £180,000 per annum. It's not huge but nevertheless it's larger than some other Collections have at their disposal. We're are always hopeful that it will increase, but in this climate, who knows?

So there a correspondence with Government departments for the arts?

We're different from the other national collections; we don't go directly to the DCMS, we go through the Arts Council. The Arts Council Collection is managed by the South Bank Centre, but is actually owned by Arts Council England, so there is a slightly 'arm's length' approach.

The Arts Council used to manage the collection and the Hayward Gallery directly, but then in 1987 they decided they wanted to be purely a funding body and no longer make direct provision, so we became part of the then, newly created, South Bank Centre, which came into being with the abolition of the GLC.

The collection represents succeeding generations of British artists, is there a perceived continuum, or do you find yourself grappling with waves of change in fashion, taste and change, and trying to maintain a steady course?

That is a difficult question and my personal feeling is that, the people who come to the acquisitions committee, are not people who are looking at fashion.

In the sense that contemporary art is somewhat like a driven animal, and its audience too?

Well, we don't buy to fill historical gaps. The aim of the Collection is to buy works at a critical point in the artist's career, when they're still affordable. Our knowledge and experience comes from working within the art world, one sees shows, reads, talk to other curators and artists. And our feeling is that this approach works. For example, we bought a Damien Hirst vitrine at a very important point in his career, just before he became world famous. We're buying because we're trying to reflect what is happening in British art at the time.

I understand. It's much more focussed on the artist, individual artists, rather than on movements and events – eruptions?

In a sense, however, we've bought a lot of video art, for example; a practice which has really grown in the past twenty years. We are looking at what artists are doing, and if we feel they're making an important contribution , they will be considered for the Collection. I suppose it's the difference between a national collection and a private collector. A private collector can buy simply because they like something. Some private collectors will look at it as a long term investment. In any collection there are works which don't get shown as much as others or are requested for loan less in the course of time. At the time you don't have the benefit of hindsight so that's why we try to look at the actual work and what the artist is doing first.

We're sitting in the ACE Collection store, where you are a few days a week. This is where galleries, museums, and others, come to look at work, and choose for exhibitions?

Yes, and we also lend to publicly funded bodies; charities, universities, libraries, and on occasions, hospitals. That is very much part of the original aims of the Arts Council Collection. There are so many people in this country who don't go into art galleries, who have not come across British art at all, so in a sense we're bringing it to them.

Works of great value?

Well, I doubt whether we would lend Francis Bacon to a hospital. We have to be realistic, the insurance would be prohibitive; and then there are the security and environmental concerns. Nevertheless we make a good body of work available for people to choose from. I think we have about twelve hundred works out on long term loan. People write to us, or phone us. Myself or one of my colleagues, would go

Installation view of *Unpopular Culture: Grayson Perry selects from the Arts Council Collection* touring exhibition at Longside Gallery, Yorkshire Sculpture Park, 2009. Photo: Jonty Wilde Courtesy ACE

and see them and talk through the security requirements; and see the areas where they want to place works of art. Our staff deliver and install the works as these borrowers don't necessarily have staff who are experienced in handling works of art. They pay a small fee for this service.

Some situations have a complete lack of security.

Well, the works are fixed to the walls very securely. They go in places where they are very visible. We talk to the potential borrower very seriously, about their responsibilities. They have to make regular checks on the condition and of course, that they're still on the walls. The works have to be fully insured by the borrower. We would never lend an un-glazed painting, unless it was a large canvas that could be hung out of reach. It may seem extraordinary, but there is very little damage. Generally people who come to us for works of art are pretty en-thusiastic and committed and they want to be able to continue to borrow from us. It improves their environment hugely and some universities who have bor-rowed from us have used it in their teaching courses.

How long do you let works out for?

They're out on long term loan for three to five years. To be honest, the demand from people wanting to borrow from the Collec-tion is infinite, as it has a substantial reputa-tion. The Collection has remained true to this idea from the very beginning. Personally I think it's a very good thing.

'Unpopular Culture', curated by Grayson Perry. Can you to describe that exhibition to me.

Grayson had done a show with Lincolnshire Museums, where he'd worked with their social history collection, and produced an exhibition called *'The Charms of Lincolnshire'*, which was shown in Lincoln and at Victoria Miro Gallery, London. It occurred to us that Grayson would be an interesting person to ask to do a show from the Collection. We invited him to the store, we talked to him, gave him our collection catalogues, made some proposals, which actually he didn't like at all.

He went away and came back with the idea; of focussing on artists before they became as famous as they have in the 'Brit Art' age. For example, when say, Kenneth Armitage made a bronze in the 1950s, it wouldn't make headline news. Now you regularly see Damien Hirst and Tracey Emin, in our national newspapers. That would not necessarily have been in the case in the '50s and '60s. Of course there was David Hockney, but in his catalogue essay Grayson says he doesn't buy the notion of the 'Swinging Sixties'.

Most of the people in this country were still living in a 1950s atmosphere. Life outside London was very everyday; people went to work, children to school, watched a bit of television. The 'Swinging Sixties' were a London phenomenon. Grayson wanted to look at a quieter time – which he describes as 'When we were more humane'. The show ends around the beginning of the 1980s with David Hepher's marvellous painting, *'Arrangement in Turquoise and Cream'*, the subject matter being ironically, Stockwell Flats, London.

George Shaw, **The End of Time**, 2008-2009.
Arts Council Collection, Southbank Centre, London
Photographer Peter White, FXP.
Courtesy Wilkinson Gallery, London

Grayson's comment was 'How can they put people in these buildings? 'The show was enormously successful, we opened it at Bexhill, at the De La Warr Pavilion, then it toured to about ten venues around the UK. We also showed it at our Longside Gallery at the Yorkshire Sculpture Park, alongside a programme of films from the BFI, which Grayson also curated. We had a fascinating two days looking at public information films in the BFI cinema.

Over the years we've done a huge amount of touring exhibitions, thematic shows. We've also done shows focussing on a single artist from our collection; people like Eduardo Paolozzi, David Hockney, and Antony Gormley's, *'Field for the British Isles'*; which was our most ambitious acquisition ever.

Yes, it's an extraordinary work. You didn't have anything to do with the 'Angel of the North'?

No.

How do you store the 'Field'?

It consists of about forty thousand figures and we store it in palettes on racks of figures and we store it in palettes on racks. It's our most loved acquisition, a wonderful work, an incredibly ambitious thing to buy which we couldn't have realised without support from the Henry Moore Foundation and The Art Fund.

What is your current programme?

We're doing a series of exhibitions called *'Flashback'*. Our first one launched last year was Bridget Riley. The rationale being to show early works from the Collection alongside more recent works lent by the artist or other collections. It helps us to see how an artist has developed and changed over the course of their career. The next one is Anish Kapoor, followed by Gary Hume, so it's quite an exciting programme. Keep watching our web site which tells you what we're doing. It is a loan collection and it's meant to be out there.

Sculpture Space

Interview with Clare Lilley,
Head Curator and Head of Programme,
The Yorkshire Sculpture Park
Recorded 29th May 2010

Cv/VAR What is your title at Yorkshire Sculpture Park?
CL I'm the Head Curator/Head of Programme, which means that I head up the direction of the programme: the exhibitions, projects, learning, and public engagement, and I oversee marketing – those teams work together very closely.
And how did you come to YSP?
Immediately before I was running galleries in North Wales at Oriel Theatr Clwyd. I ran three spaces – a public gallery in a large theatre/cinema complex, a primarily commercial gallery in the same place, and a community space in the town library. It was a hard mix, and a steep learning curve. Before that I was an intern at Cornerhouse, Manchester; my first real work with contemporary art while I researched my MPhil at Manchester University. Medieval architecture was a passion at university, and I had worked as an assistant to the curator of an amazing medieval art exhibition at the Royal Academy. However, I fairly quickly became engrossed with modern and contemporary art. I was brought up north of Liverpool and came from a family with no interest in art; around the age of 15 I started stealing off to the Walker Art Gallery in Liverpool. At that time they had both the John Moores and Peter Moores exhibitions. The Peter Moores

exhibitions were of contemporary sculpture, and there I first saw artists like Deacon, Flanagan and Cragg. Those experiences really pulled me into art and took me on to do an art history degree at Manchester University.
So you didn't actually do a curator training?
No, I started an MPhil at Manchester on Georgia O'Keeffe, the American painter – it was interesting because it was totally unstructured, more like a mini-PhD. I was encouraged to do it by my supervisor, the excellent art historian, Andrew Causey. At the same time I worked for Sue Grayson Ford at Cornerhouse, very soon after it opened. Sue was fantastic; she had been the first Director of the Serpentine Gallery, when it principally showed new and emerging artists. I was given some very rich opportunities by her and worked with some great artists and on great projects, including Kiefer, Baselitz, Penck and Immendorf and other international artists. I was also commissioned to do some research for Sue's husband, Colin Ford, who was the founding director of the National Museum of Photography in Bradford and who curated the exhibition, Masterpieces of Twentieth Century Photography, on which I worked. Those were extraordinary experiences, very exciting. A whole world opened up that was so different to what I'd known.
Theatr Clwyd emerges and disappears and emerges again?
I've lost touch with it now, but it was an interesting proposition. Theatr Clwyd was one of those 1970s social and civic enterprises, of which there were many in Wales; there's a gallery or theatre pretty

much within reach of every small town and they were established with a very clear quality of life agenda. In terms of education, people in Wales are extremely fortunate because of the fantastic support system that comes out of an entrenched liberal philosophy. It's integrated in a very quiet way, but it's there within the fabric of society. I ran a space in the library, which in many ways was really difficult, but the notion of art being woven into ordinary life has always been really important to me.

So when I saw the post of Arts Co-ordinator advertised at Yorkshire Sculpture Park, I desperately wanted to be here. Right from my first visit (with Sue Grayson Ford), I knew it was unusual. It was an organisation that didn't have the same barriers, in terms of contemporary art, that many museums and galleries have. There was literally no front door then, and how you mediate or experience art in the landscape at YSP is incredibly interesting – the potential is gigantic and is still growing.

You've got a lot of space.

Yes, we've got over five hundred acres of 18th century designed landscape. When I first came we owned around fifteen acres, had no indoor space, and used about one hundred acres to show sculpture. The estate was the campus for Bretton Hall College, which had been established by the important educationalist Sir Alec Clegg, just after World War II. His philosophy, linked to that of Harry Thubron in the north-east, developed from Bauhaus and Beuysian ideas – direct contact with materials, processes,

and artists – about self expression, intellect, expansion. The Sculpture Park was founded by Peter Murray, who had taught at post-graduate level in the college and these have been the driving ethos of YSP, right from its beginning in 1977. It's one with which everyone who works here, who stays the distance, becomes enmeshed. You could say that the great art for everyone's agenda has been played out here for over thirty years – and that includes for artists, who get great opportunities and support here. As well as the five hundred acres, which as of this year also includes two lakes and a nature reserve, there are four galleries, a visitor centre with spaces, a chapel, a boathouse and lab space, a learning tent, plus very well equipped workshops. It's quite a mix.

We could bring David Nash in here, whose exhibition at YSP just opened (28th May 2010), because he was here early on.

Yes, he was first at YSP in 1979 as part of the Wood exhibition. I think it's true to say that one of the reasons David wanted to be here then was a shared interest in the social and personal possibilities of visual art and he fed into the ideas and philosophy of this place. The college has been an important thread running through the development of YSP, though they ran as very separate entities. Eventually the college was taken over by the University of Leeds who pulled out a few years ago, leaving a huge block of empty buildings, which have now been purchased by Wakefield MDC, giving us some opportunity for further capital development. When I first came here in

1991, none of that had happened yet, but in the same year we built a pavilion structure and made a Lynn Chadwick show there. That was the first purpose-built gallery; I think it had planning permission for four years and it ended up staying for thirteen, before it went off to be a bar in Marbella.

What is the funding support for YSP?

It's a mixed bag and it's taken a huge amount of work to get to the level that it is. Just under half our income is from Arts Council England, Wakefield MDC and West Yorkshire Grants; the rest is earned income from trusts and foundations, sponsorship, retail from the shop and cafés, art workshops and art sales, and donations. Also, in 2000 we acquired our main holding of land, the Longside valley, together with a number of buildings, and over the last ten years have worked very hard to pull the estate back together so that now we have stewardship of the five hundred acres and have developed a small cultural industries cluster.

Tenancy and rentals income is therefore part of the mix. We currently have an audience of around 250,000 each year and unlike many regional galleries, that audience generates a significant income – so for that reason (and because we're such enthusiasts!) there's a great impetus to keep it increasing. Our art sales also generate real income – from artist limited editions to high-end sculpture sales, so we work pretty hard to expand and deepen that collector base. It's a great range: in the same day we could be talking to a collector who's flown in by heli-copter, and to a college student, or an asylum seeker involved with a programme here. Over the last few years, fundraising for capital has been significant, we've raised and invested around £15 million over that time and in fact we're currently in the process of developing a new education centre, converting some quite grand 18th century kennels, that has been gifted to us by Rushbond, the development company that is converting the Bretton Hall mansion into a five star hotel. The hotel and its adjacent buildings will be a very good thing for YSP and offer yet more opportunities.

I noticed Roger Evans' name in the David Nash exhibition?

Individual sponsors have been important all the way, none more so than Roger who has been extremely generous and is a great friend to YSP. Henry Moore was probably the first; he gave a modest amount of cash, but his advice and other support was fundamental.

Have you a direct relation with the Henry Moore Foundation?

The Foundation has been a crucial supporter for many years, not just in terms of sculpture loans and financially, but also in terms of its staff and trustees giving good counsel. Since 1994 we've had a holding of Henry Moore sculptures in the 96 acre country park.

Of course that's very appropriate, because of Moore's early support of the Park, and also because he was born in Castleford which is just a few miles away. This is the landscape of his boyhood and he particularly liked the

Country Park. It is one of the roughest areas of land with fantastic views across the valley; there are sheep – there are many synergies. And of course, Barbara Hepworth was born and raised in Wakefield, and the Hepworth Estate is also an extremely important supporter in terms of lending work, particularly the seminal group of Hepworth sculptures called 'The Family of Man'. Sir Alan Bowness, who until very recently, ran the Hepworth Estate, was also director of Tate and of the Henry Moore Foundation and the relationship with Tate, from which we also have significant loans, has contributed to the Park's success today. Sir Alan has been instrumental in many ways and actually I think his influence on contemporary art, especially on sculpture in Britain in the post-war period and on visual art development in the regions, is seriously undervalued. Certainly he has valued the development of an institution in the UK that worked with sculpture in the open-air.

It must be wonderful for artists, sculptors, to work in this relatively free and open environment.

It's really fantastic, but it's a very demanding place as well: incredibly challenging for artists of all ages and experience. I've seen very eminent artists literally blanch when they've looked at what we propose – two of our galleries are also very big spaces. As well as engagement with the public in a very particular way, we give artists opportunities to do things they couldn't anywhere else.

They tend to work on site, or do they bring works in?

Both. The first exhibition we held in the Underground Gallery was with William Turnbull, we brought in his work from around the UK and Europe. In 1973 when he was in his fities, Bill had a major retrospective at Tate, but never before had he the opportunity to make such a complete statement inside and outdoors. I worked with him to really create a project that worked across the environments, and that did justice to his practice over a very long career.

One of the things we care about here, and generally it seems to go unspoken, is aesthetic value, about how you can best show a work in a given situation; and it simply isn't possible to install works outdoors in the way that you can in a gallery. It's almost anti-museological and quite a difficult thing to articulate, but it is a way of working that we've developed over time that carefully considers balance and scale and distance, relationship to environment and object, line and volume. I believe paying heed to these issues help make this a place that people love.

Also, we have an incredible team and they work very hard, even though, like me, many have been here for a long time. YSP gets into your blood and alongside that is a fantastic sense of trust between colleagues; all the people in the office and trading company, the gardeners and estates team, our security team, and exceptional technicians, we know we can depend on each other to a very high degree. That's something artists really value too and because our staff are so dedicated and knowledgeable, it's possible for artists to realise complicated and complex projects and to feel supported in a pretty special way.

How do you pick and choose and formulate a programme?

To some degree, and particularly outdoors, it comes back to how you think something is going to work, but essentially we have a programme of 'big' exhibitions, and they're always monographs – the mainstay of the programme, attracting big audiences. Most often they are indoor/outdoor shows so we are of course interested in those artists who can handle outdoor spaces.

We like working with artists who feel pushed by this place, by what it offers and its context, and whose projects therefore develop in exciting or unexpected ways. The same goes for artists who make smaller or ephemeral projects. Over the years we've introduced many artists to this country, or have curated significant statements by those who are well known; people like James Turrell and Andy Goldsworthy. The challenge here is important and really interesting. By their nature, our major shows are expensive so they need to be able to live for six months or more; therefore they need to contain a richness that warrants repeat visits, so that visitors find more on each viewing. That's especially the case with work outdoors, which can develop and breathe in truly wonderful ways with the seasons, weather or time of day.

I suppose it's true to say that many of our shows have clear connections to the natural world, but that isn't always the case and nor is it necessary. However, there are definitely projects we want to do, particularly during the summer months, where there is a kind of dialogue between artwork and viewer, and between gallery and landscape. Where there is a really thorough, enjoyable, gutsy statement by an artist. So for that reason, yes, we are looking to artists who can deal with this kind of landscape, and not all can or want to. But we also make masses of projects with artists who might have different concerns, or whose practice is ephemeral, based around text, sound, performance or movement. In those cases, we make contact with artists who we think are interesting, who could contribute something to the place and to the audience, who might be able to articulate a given area of interest and to gain something within their own practice in the process. So we begin a conversation and see where it leads – sometimes nowhere, sometimes to small interventions over a period of time, sometimes very quickly, sometimes taking years.

While we commission permanent works infrequently (so far only LeWitt, Turrell, Goldsworthy and Nash), we enable a lot of new work: Dalziel + Scullion, John Newling, Bethan Huws, Brass Art, Sarah Staton, Alec Finlay, Brandon Ballengée, are some that come to mind. We usually have at least one Visiting Artist at any one time, who stays in our flat and develops work over a period of time, often a project that involves direct interaction with the audience. Those projects enable a really particular, meaningful engagement. So these strands, that include exhibitions of objects in the galleries and outdoors, ephemeral works and actions, live

Henry Moore **Draped Seated Woman** (1957-58)
At the Yorkshire Sculpture Park
Photo: Jonty Wilde Courtesy YSP

art, situations and processes, weave together into a fairly complex and very interesting matrix.

And knowing the artists?

Relationships with some artists develop over many years. James Turrell first stayed here and made drawings in 1993, but his major exhibition and the opening of his Skyspace took place in 2006. We first met Jaume Plensa in 1998 and over the years there have been points at which we've touched base, had conversations. And then you get to a point, it was the same with David Nash, that you know the time is right, and the time for Jaume will be 2011. It's really hard to put your finger on why it's that point; the artist's practice and their other commitments, the rhythm and diversity of the programme; sometimes expediency related to transport or funding, especially now we're increasingly dependent on private sponsors. So developing relationships with dealers and collectors is also a feature.

It's a kind of jigsaw of pieces that at a moment in time you can lock together. At the moment I'm having fairly serious conversations with more than a dozen artists from this country, India, Portugal, Italy, South Africa and more. My sense is that all of them would be good here, big and small projects – the trick is figuring out capacity, timing, partnerships and funding.

What about public programmes, schools for instance?

We have a massive learning programme, touching most of the schools in the area and many schools and colleges around the country, plus third age learners, pre-school groups etc; about 40,000 people come through the learning programme every year. Often they are engaged in hands-on work, but engagement here is considered to be incredibly important and goes on in every area – from dawn birdsong events to study days, from welding workshops and pond-dipping, to artists' lectures or walking projects.

We also work with social service teams in Wakefield, Barnsley and elsewhere and have projects that involve young offenders, prisoners, those dealing with substance abuse, mental health issues, and a long-term programme of working with asylum seekers and refugees. So very specific work with acute concern, in addition to the huge schools and colleges programme. And we have particular higher education relationships with York St. John and The University of Huddersfield, ranging from work experience placements to PhD research. All of the learning contact work is delivered by artists, so we're also a fairly significant employer in that respect.

The Sculpture Park has been here for thirty years?

Yes, that's a generation: we've been here for the entire lives of children, who think it's completely normal to have a sculpture park on your doorstep, who are surprised to find there aren't more when they move away. That's fantastic and is an indication of how the Park is a real and true thing in the lives of people. We have a Memory Project which started in 2007 for the thirtieth anniversary year, where we invited people to log memories of YSP on the website. We've had thousands of responses and frequently they reference birth, relationships, anniversaries, celebration, death - the stuff of life –vwith YSP as a place that's relevant and about which many people are very passionate. You've probably seen we've got a walkway that leads into the Centre, called the *Walk of Art.* It was a good fundraiser, but more than that, it's a place where people could have their names set into the fabric of the place, forever, or at least for a very long time. YSP is very much a part of people's lives, and special in a very particular way.

James Turrell **Deer Shelter**
At the Yorkshire Sculpture Park
Photo: Jonty Wilde Courtesy YSP

Renovation and Revision

Director Dr Christopher Brown,
on the development of
The Ashmolean Museum, Oxford.

Cv/VAR When did you join The Ashmolean Museum?
CB In 1998. I came as director from the National Gallery in London.
We're going to focus on the renovation programme that transformed the museum. Were you the driving force behind that?
Yes.
And how did this come about, was there a great need for a renovation?
I worked for many years at the National Gallery as the curator of Dutch and Flemish paintings; subsequently as the chief curator, which is essentially the deputy director post at the National Gallery. And my interest in coming to The Ashmolean, which was a museum I knew well, having been an undergraduate and graduate at Oxford, was to raise the profile of the institution; to really look at how the collections were displayed and to improve that. This was discussed at the interview and was the understanding I had in taking the job: we were going to undertake a significant development of the museum.
The Ashmolean is a very old institution, what sort of state did you find it in? Were there particular aspects that you felt could be improved?
It is. It opened in Oxford in 1683, it's the oldest public museum in this country and, we have reason to think, the oldest public museum in Europe. So it is a very important institution in terms of the

history of museums. It's very important to make the point right at the beginning that, although it's part of the University of Oxford, it has never been restricted only to the members of the University. It's always been a public museum from the moment it opened. Not of course in this building, but one in Broad Street in Oxford.
And when you arrived as director?
The situation in 1998 was my predecessor, who remarkably was called Christopher White, had begun to develop the museum as a much more public facing institution and he had undertaken quite a large scheme, which involved going under the forecourt, to provide facilities that any modern museum needs. There was as lecture theatre, workshops, a café. A couple of galleries were also built in an internal courtyard. However my own sense was that something more radical was needed, particularly at the back of the museum. When I was appointed in 1998, the first thing I undertook was a master plan of the building.
What did this reveal?
The master plan threw up a whole series of problems with the 1894 building which had been put on the back of the 1845 building. The original building is by Charles Cockerell in 1845. In 1894 Arthur Evans, who was the great excavator of Knossos, Crete; using the money provided by Charles Fortnum, who made his fortune from Fortnum and Mason, built a large section onto the back of the 1845 building, to house the very large archaeological collections which were coming into the museum at that time. We identified that

area of 1890s additions, and small subsequent additions, as the problem.

What kind of problems?

The problems were no kind of environmental control at all; so, for example, you were unable to show any of the textile collection at all. Any organic material is very much affected by changes in relative humidity, so if you can't control relative humidity you can't show them. Light is important as well, but it's essentially a matter of RH. The second problem was the very poor use of space. These were late Victorian buildings that used half the potential space; they were rather light industrial structures, which has come to be known as 'Evans sheds'. They only used the space half way up. Then there were lots of changes of level, which was very difficult in terms of disability access legislation. But also just difficult in terms of moving about the building. There was no loading bay, no education centre, we were unable to properly welcome school-age visitors.

So a whole range of difficulties.

A whole series of technical problems. In the first year when I came, I tried to get those buildings to work a bit better and I wondered whether we could retain them, but just re-model them. So I looked at the lighting, the labelling and the displays and we made some significant changes there. However in the winter of '99/2000, a roof of one of those buildings was partially blown off in a gale. Then I realised, not only were they working very badly, but also there were real maintenance issues to be dealt with. It was in early 2000 that we started planning what to demolish,

which at that moment was sixty percent of the museum. The 1845 building is tall and thin, it is one gallery deep, so when you entered through the very grand portico it was to one gallery.

In 1894 Evans bought the site at the back of The Ashmolean and developed that into a series of five pitched roof sheds, which ran east to west along the back of the existing building. They were public galleries for display of the large archaeological collection which was coming in from the 1890s to 1900. We were proposing in 2000 to demolish sixty percent of the building, the 1890s bit, and to redevelop the whole site. We did that and then went down a floor and connected up to the lower level of the 1845 building and then built the whole thing back on six floors.

That is very ambitious, how was it integrated with what was kept of the old building?

It was a very difficult architectural issue for two particular reasons: first of all, and as you can see very clearly here, that is the Classics Centre opposite; we're built on all four sides by the University, so we couldn't expand the site. Secondly, we could only go down one floor because of the water table in this part of Oxford, and we could only go up to this height, because it was an absolutely reasonable condition of being granted listed building consent: that you shouldn't see the new building from the outside. It was therefore a very interesting and a very difficult architectural problem, which we think has been solved extremely well by Rick Mather.

How did you choose your architect?

We had a competition in the normal way.

The client, of course, was the museum, but the client was also the University. Essentially the University was the formal client here, and it has RIBA rules about how you do these things. We had an architectural; competition, which was won in the summer of 2002.

What attracted you to Rick Mather's proposal?

I knew his work very well already at the Dulwich Picture Gallery, where I had been a Trustee. And indeed John Sainsbury, who has been one of the great supporters of this scheme, was chairman of the Dulwich Trustees at the time, so there was a kind of team there. What I wanted from the outset was a modern building, I wanted a contemporary building; a building of 2009. I didn't want a pastiche building. If you do that the issue is essentially one of transition; from the 1845 building which has quite rich internal decoration, elaborate cornices and doors, staircases etc., managing the transition from that to the new building. This was a big, sixty million pound project, and lots of people wanted to do it. Most of them suggested a glass and steel extension on the back. The key to what Rick's done in the transition, is that you go through on the flat on the ground and the first floor, from the old to the new building.

What that actually means is that the floor arrangement of the old building then necessarily defines the arrangement of the new building. Between the ground and first floor is a height of six metres, carrying the height to the new gallery. Then you break off to three metre high galleries either side. If you then move to the atrium and look to your left you see three six metre high galleries, as it were, stacked on one another.

So the architectural rhythm of the building is six metres, three metres, six metres, all the way through. That's the basic grid on which it works. There are two other important aspects to this. The first is, if you open up a lower ground level as a principal public floor, you have to bring light down there; you can't have any kind of dingy basement effect. You've got to have it well lit. So Rick created two great staircases, a central staircase which steps back as it goes up, opening up in a funnel effect, with a huge skylight of thirteen metres at the top, bringing light all the way down through the building and to the lower ground floor. There's another fine staircase, not quite as big, which has side light from a huge wall of glass. So there's a definition of the new by the old building.

What materials were used in the new building?

There's a continuation of materials from the old building which is important. The first public gallery you come into, right up to the atrium, is made with English limestone, Portland stone, that connects into English limestone in the old building.

This was the architect's suggestion?

Yes, but there was a lot of discussion. Rick was appointed to the project in 2002, he was personally very involved in this scheme, and then in 2004 we appointed Metaphor, a design company led by Stephen Greenberg, who helped us with the layout and design of the individual galleries. From that stage it was a three

The cascading staircase lit at night
© Andy Matthews
Courtesy The Ashmolean Museum

part conversation. The architectural competition was held in the summer of 2002. From the very beginning this project was supported by Lord Sainsbury. We made a complex application to the Heritage Lottery Fund, and we received fifteen million pounds from there in the summer of 2004. It was really at that point we knew we were in business, it was a key moment. We broke ground in September 2006, when we began the demolition of the old building, and we opened to the public in November 2009. The Queen opened the museum on December 2nd 2009 and I'm glad to tell you that this Tuesday (21st September), we had our millionth visitor, in ten months since the re-opening, which is very remarkable for a museum outside London.

Yes, that is amazing. Can we touch on the collection?

Of course the point of the enterprise is not the building but the display of collection; that is what the whole thing is about, what it arises from. The collections of The Ashmolean are the best, the most comprehensive for art and archaeology, of any museum in this country, outside London. In my view they were not punching their weight; not enough of the collections were being shown, nor were they being shown well. So as well as increasing the number of objects on view, we also re-displayed them in a way that makes them more understandable and attractive to a broad public.

In the new building there are thirty nine new galleries. Thirty five are the permanent collection, four are temporary exhibition galleries. There's an education centre, a loading bay, teaching rooms, store rooms; there are conservation studios. There is the new rooftop restaurant and of course administrative offices, and we're sitting in my new office on the top of this block. There's a connection through from the building to The Cast Gallery. We have a very important collection of casts here which are housed in their own building, which is accessed separately.

Establishing so many new galleries must have given considerable opportunities to explore?

Clearly when you do something on this scale, you can think very radically about how you display your collections. This, as I said, was demolishing sixty percent of the museum and looking also at the historic building, so it was a very rare opportunity to think about how one should display the collections in a more effective manner. When planning this we knew we going to have six floors, we didn't know how the internal spaces were going to work.

I convened a group of curators. Like all major museums we have departments within it. Here we have five departments: Eastern art; Western Art; Antiquities, which is the archaeological collection; Numismatics: the Coin Room, and the Cast Gallery. We gathered together a curatorial group from across the museum and asked them to consider how we should display the collections. They went away for quite a long time and came back to say: there are six floors; one is for temporary exhibitions, so we'll put Western art in a gallery and Eastern art in a gallery. I said "I'm not entirely sure how to do this, because I come from a painting gallery: The National Gallery, and frankly, hanging pictures is a complete doddle compared to doing these kind of collections." But I knew we should not follow the conventional path of departmental collections: this is the area for Western art, this for Eastern art, this area for archaeology.

It seems to me, if you display your collections in that traditional departmental way, it is absolutely inevitable that you stress cultural difference, rather than cultural contact and exchange. It creates barriers between civilisations.

But that is The British Museum way?

It is the traditional way and I can come back to that. The point about The Ashmolean's collections is they are very varied; from 8000 BC to the present day. From almost all civilisations, though not

Ashmolean main staircase © Greg Smolonski / Photovibe
Courtesy of the Ashmolean Museum / University of Oxford

much from South America or Australasia, and of very high quality; of British Museum quality but not its quantity. So if you want to establish narratives which make useful cultural links, it's much easier to do that in a collection of this scale, rather than a collection on the scale of The British Museum.

What came from the discussions?

We had a whole series of lengthy and interesting seminars, discussions within the museum. And of course, because this is part of a university, we brought in our colleagues from the Archaeology department, the Classics department, Oriental Studies and so on. And we had a whole series of seminars about how you do this. Perhaps one way to illustrate it, as an example of a discussion; we have a very important sculpture from Gandhara, (modern Pakistan/Afghanistan), from first century AD, of a Buddha wearing a Roman toga. We also have Gandharan sculptures which show the clear influence of Roman sarcophagi. What you've got there is a civilisation on the very edge of the classical world, with a new religion

Nandí Granite, Deccan or South India, 16th-17th century, H 55.9 x L 69.9 x W 40.6 cm.
© Ashmolean Museum, University of Oxford

coming from the East. A real point where the two civilisations meet to produce the absolutely beautiful and remarkable phenomenon.

If you show it in the traditional way, in the Eastern Art Department, then you show Gandharan sculpture with traditional Indian and Chinese artefacts, all of which we have in the collection. Clearly you make the point that this is related to a new Buddhist style of subject matter. However, if you do it like that. you entirely miss the classical dimension, So the issue is how you display the Gandharan sculpture to make known to the public its classical heritage, but also to place it in the context of later Buddhist art.

How have you introduced these links and themes?

You come in on the ground floor; that floor is devoted to the ancient world, from 8000 BC to the fall of Rome. You enter the big six metre gallery, which we call the Orientation Gallery, which introduces you to the geography and chronology of the ancient world. There is a case in the middle which is all about the transport of people and things. There is an important point here that cultural styles moved about with the people, more than you may imagine.

You then turn left, because everybody in public buildings in this country turns left; we know that from our research. From the Orientation Gallery you go into the Aegean World. Here we have our great Minoan collection, the most significant collection outside of Herakleon in Crete, as well as a great Cycladic collection: the finest group of Cycladic sculptures outside Athens. You follow through the Aegean World, Ancient Near East, Pre-Historic Cyprus, Pre-Historic Europe, Greece, Rome, Gandhara, India, China,

Japan. Gandhara is placed between Rome and India, establishing that profound relationship between Gandharan Art and Classical art, and then of course Buddhist art. So there is a sequence and a sort of narrative through that floor of the building. I may add we are presently working on a new display of our Egyptian collection for 2011.

Who founded the collections?

The founding collections were made by a family called Tradescant, and they showed these collections in their house in Lambeth, South London, in the 1630s. Many visitors to the house recorded their visits, invariably saying that, visiting the Tradescant Museum, as it was known in Lambeth, was like going round the world in a day.

What a lovely way of putting it.

It has a very nice resonance with the way we've laid out the collection. Going to the next floor we move from the Fall of Rome to the low Middle Ages, and then on to the High Middle Ages to the early Modern World. So the collection is laid out on those three principal floors. On the lower ground floor the galleries are arranged more thematically: a gallery devoted to the history of the museum, a gallery for our numismatic collection, which has been very well done and is very popular. There are also two galleries devoted to the history and ethics of conservation; the only ones, I think, of their kind in the UK. The third floor is for temporary exhibitions, with the Pre-Raphaelite exhibition at the moment. Conservation studios, administrative offices and a restaurant are situated on the top floor. That's the building and arrangement of the collections.

Your own specialism has been Flemish and Dutch painting. Has working on this major project at The Ashmolean removed you from your research?

Well I'm always surprised when people say, 'It must be very difficult being director, you have very little time for research on your own subject.' But in a way that is the deal. Becoming director I knew I was going to develop The Ashmolean, and so I became a builder for a good number of years. You simply have to put aside your research and your own work for that period of time. And of course in my case, moving from The National Gallery to The Ashmolean; there are good Dutch and Flemish paintings here. I have strengthened that aspect with individual loans of Rembrandt and other major artists. I am entirely relaxed about it, it's what I chose to do at this stage in my career. I would have been happy to stay at The National Gallery, but I had this opportunity and knew what it involved; the undertaking of a great project at The Ashmolean, and very deliberately made that choice. However, I went to a Rubens conference last week, so I keep my hand in occasionally.

Creative Dialogues

Interview with Vincent Honoré
Curator of David Roberts Art Foundation

Cv/VAR Here we are at the David Roberts Art Foundation in Great Tichfield Street. You're just setting up a show, tell me what it's about?

VH The show is with a guest curator. One of the programmes of the foundation, and an important mission of the Foundation, is to support independent curators; curators who we think have a specific tone of voice in contemporary art. Often those curators propose their first exhibition in London here. '**History of Art, The**' is a proposal by Mihnea Mircan, who is a Romanian curator. He is known for the Romanian Pavilion at the Venice Biennale three years ago; one of the best pavilions I've seen. This will be his first exhibition in London. The exhibition questions the structures of artists and their relation to art history, and how from the beginning, artists can position their work in future or potential history, or how they can navigate and manipulate art history.

Is he himself, a practising artist?

He's a curator, not an artist.

It's an interesting distinction. How do you choose projects?

We don't accept proposals, it's only by invitation. We select curators from projects we have seen. We thought it would make sense to present a curators' series in London. It is an innovative way to position art works. I didn't know Mihnea Mircan before I invited him to propose a show for the foundation. It's important to stress that, in order to be as open as we can with this series. The first curator was Cylena Simonds. She's a London based curator who was working at INIVA, where she presented a Cuban art exhibition. She did an exhibition at the Foundation about service industry and artists. The second curator was Raimundas Malasauskas from Lithuania who was based in New York, now in Paris. He made an exhibition around J.G.Ballard, with Ryan Gander, Mario Garcia Torres, Rosalind Nashashibi and Gintaras Didziapetris.

Not the same as the Gagosian show 'Crash!'

Not at all, not illustrative of Crash by J.G.Ballard. The works were infused by Ballard, but not illustring his style or novels. The third curator is Mihnea Mircan and the fourth, in the Spring will be Mathieu Copeland from France.

Each show runs for about three months?

Yes.

Do you produce a catalogue for it?

We tend not to produce catalogues. It's not so much a matter of money as that we are a small team, and there is a problem of delegating time. I think in the art world we tend to produce too many books. I want to be focused, and when we need to publish we do it. We produce leaflets and booklets, I would not call them catalogues.

Your own dialogue with the curator, Do you trust his or her choice of artist, or do you sometimes moderate what is presented?

We invite curators a year and a half before the exhibition. It's not much time but enough to develop a project. They come to the gallery for a site visit, to develop their concept. They work really closely with us so we follow the project from A to Z. I work with a curator the way I work with an artist. Trying to ease the project materially and intellectually, sometimes my role is to allow a bit of distance between the project and the curator, so he or she can see it from a distance and it can be edited. It's the same with the artist. We are keen to work closely with our collaborators, be they artists or curators.

This thing about histories and where an artist fits is something the artists have always been aware of.

Especially with contemporary art. Having said that, the curators are totally free to propose what they wish. They can work with work from the collection, but they have no obligation to use our collection. It's very important they remain independent. Their freedom is something we are very keen on in the Foundation.

And artists are happy with this way of working?

I hope so.

You started at the Palais de Tokyo?

Yes and then I worked at Tate Modern.

What changes did you experience, in ways of working?

I'm not sure how you mean. It depends whether you're talking about an institution or a Foundation or a gallery. I think it's more about situations than positions, as curators or collectors, or artists. It depends in which situation the artist is working. For example, some big institutions think they have the obligation to draw large audiences to justify the grants they receive.

To do that, to attract as many people as they can, they tend to do spectacular exhibitions. Spectacular because the artists are well known, or because it's a big installation. As a consequence they tend not to be as experimental as they could have been. And some artists can hardly show any more in the big institutions, because they would not bring a sufficient audience. In the smaller foundations, we can propose a space for artists and curators, a dialogue; a place where dialogue and change can happen. Then again, the independent or alternative spaces we used to have are not as vivid as they used to be. They simply cannot survive, they cannot find a place, they don't have enough budget, etc. So we are seeing a lot of short term projects, but time is important for artists and curators. Nowadays, independent initiatives, are more and more going underground, or on the periphery of big cities. There are less alternatives for artists and curators of where to work. Foundations may have this role, which we try to provide here. Others such as Nomas in Rome and Kadist in Paris operate in the same direction than DRAF.

The David Roberts Foundation has built a considerable collection of works.

We have 1,650 works by 350 artists at the moment, acquired over a period of ten years.

And the range is not just contemporary?

I would say 80% of works in the collection have been created after 1995; then we have a small collection of modern art: including Rodchenko and Man Ray, possibly about 5% of the collection; the rest is made of post-war art, with

Exhibition Oscar Tuazon, *That's Not Made for That,*
David Roberts Art Foundation, 2009
Installation view with works by Oscar Tuazon and Jim Goldberg
Image: Damien Griffiths, 2009

Lichtenstein, Andy Warhol, Peter Blake, just to name a few.

Is the collection shown, or can it be drawn on for exhibitions?

Absolutely. At the moment the collection is not shown, most of the works remain in store. Having said that, we are lending works. The work by Mona Hatoum you saw at The Royal Academy is a work from the collection. We are lending Rosemarie Trockel to Zürich, Kris Martin is going to Grasse. We are lending a lot. From time to time at the Foundation we are including works from the collection; recently Hans Peter Feldmann, Cyprien Gaillard, Ulla van Brandenburg, Yayoi Kusama and George Condo. We show works from the collection when it makes sense to show those works. Our goal is not to promote the collection, it's to do exhibitions and artistic projects. If it makes sense to use a work from the collection, of course we do it. In the future, by 2011/2012, we hope to have another space here in London, where more of the collection will be shown in a larger space.

The Foundation also maintains artists' studios?

We manage seven studios. At the moment we own three buildings in London: one is the Foundation, the second is for storage. The third is a building in Camden which we turned into, what we call, a production unit. There are seven artists' studios; a flat given for artists and curators working with the foundation. There is a company, Camden Town Unlimited, which takes care of creative industries such as design, fashion and architecture. Eventually the building will become another gallery where we will introduce more works from the collection.

Coming back to yourself. You are based in Paris, and come here for projects. Do you work there?

Yes, I'm still an independent curator, so I have other activities. Having said that, the Foundation is the main project I'm managing at the moment. But yes, I'm writing and doing exhibitions externally. It's a good thing to do, it brings a lot to me and it brings a lot to the Foundation as well.

Independent Curator

Interview recorded with James Putnam at Black's Private Members Club in Dean Street W1

Cv/VAR I notice that the opening page on your website proclaims, "All art was once contemporary". This suggests that you don't believe in separated areas between ancient and contemporary.

JP This is a notion that I've become interested in. Before I started work in contemporary art I worked for ten years in the British Museum as a more conventional curator of historical material. I was in charge of looking after the ancient Egyptian collection. I was very interested in that, but I was somewhat disappointed that the world of contemporary art and the historic world of the museum were so distanced. I found there was an opportunity there to bring them together, by doing what's since been called intervention shows. That was, bringing contemporary art into the British Museum. That's how I started.

So there was a loosening of boundaries?

I guess with most of my projects. I get a lot out of them, and I think the artists develop their work in these collaborations. The research into history and various historical artefacts, which often leads them into a new track in the work they're doing. It's been very fruitful in that respect. My curatorial practice is quite different from a lot of other curators who install art in so- called white space galleries. I have also worked in those spaces, but I do prefer the historical spaces where it's possible to interweave art with the architecture and artefacts, which I feel brings both things to another dimension. It injects the often rather staid museum space with a new energy.

What about aspects of the presentation. Can you define qualities you bring to the staging of an event or exhibition?

I am very aware of the exhibition as an event. Sometimes there's a performance for the opening, there are ways of expanding the thing from being a rather static presentation. I'm interested in that and how it develops.

Can we talk about the exhibition 'Hysteria' by Mat Collishaw, which you curated at the Freud Museum Hampstead in 2009. I found it strange and intriguing. How did you meet Mat?

I met him when he was going out with Tracey Emin. I did a project with Tracey for the British Museum and kept in contact; I'd been following his work. In the past few years he's really blossomed in what he's doing. I liked the work and invited him to do a project at the Freud Museum. Previously I had invited him to participate at the Venice Biennale, along with Paul Fryer. He was also in the Mythologies show which I curated with Ben Tufnell at the Haunch of Venison last year. So yes, I'd known him, liked his work and thought he was a good person to work with.

You've curated several exhibitions at the Freud Museum.

Yes, the first one was with Sophie Calle back in 1999, where she exhibited part of her collection and made little text labels that went round the museum. I developed a relationship with the Freud Museum from that time, and I try and do an exhibition every year there. There are certain criteria one has to follow: it has to be relevant to Freud, some writing of Freud's or some part of his collection. It's usually a combination of me talking with the artist and the curators of the Freud Museum, getting some of their specialist knowledge and steering the artist toward the project, relevant to some aspect of Freud.

A particular feature of the show was the animatronics, intricate settings that activated in timed cycles.

I think you're referring to the Zoetrope, a kind of animated sculpture, or rather a device, that produces an illusion of action for a series of small figures on a spinning base. He was making one of these for a show in Berlin and made a smaller version for the Freud Museum. This shows imp-like figures smashing eggs, spearing snails and throwing rocks at butterflies. This relates to childhood cruelty and was installed in Anna Freud's room as she was the founder of child psychology.

From the title I gather the main theme of the exhibition was about Charcot's investigation of hysteria?

Yes, above Freud's couch there's a print of the neurologist Jean Charcot with a hysterical woman, and Mat said he was very interested in the theme of hysteria and looking at the archives where Charcot had published this research. That was the central theme, but there was also this idea of childhood cruelty to animals which comes out in the Zoetrope. I was pleased he developed so much work for the exhibition.

You've just produced an exhibition in Milan, is there a difference in the audiences there and here; the kind of responses you get in London and Europe?

I think they're more serious in a way. The contemporary art scene in London is far more fashion orientated, media savvy. So if there's a buzz going around; if it's a hot show, it'll be flooded with people. In Italy you have to work quite hard to build up your audiences; to attract people into the spaces. Openings are less well attended there than they usually are in London.

A more haughty taste?

Perhaps. In London it's so trend conscious, but in Milan they're more reserved. In many openings they don't even have any alcohol. In fact this place where we're talking, Black's, helped me with the Venice Biennale. They built a bar there which was a kind of art work. It became a very good social focus for young people throughout the summer. You have to integrate that so people can meet and discuss what they've seen, rather than the constrained atmosphere of a rather serious gallery.

I followed that model with the Milan show we've just done called 'Wonderland'. I worked on that with Bridget Hugo, who constructs bars from found objects as part of her practice.

You are an independent curator, how do you interface with institutions, museums or galleries?

Sometimes you approach them with a project you think will work in their space, or they come to you to say they like a certain exhibition, can you do

Mat Collishaw **Garden of Un-Earthly Delights** 2009
Steel, aluminium, resin, plaster and led lights
75 x 75 x 150cm Courtesy of the Artist

seven artists, just choosing one or two works, depending on the size of the gallery.

Are you always looking?

Yes, sometimes artists invite me to their studios. I go and see the work. I don't often go to the degree shows, but like a lot of people I'm on the lookout for new artists whose work needs promoting in some way, so I can help them. I try to do a mixture of working with established artists and emerging artists.

You hold sessions here at Black's.

Yes, the salons. I started doing these with Sasha Craddock, the curator of the Bloomberg Space, who's also a well known writer and broadcaster. We thought of this nice idea to have a salon, where we invite artists, musicians, scientists, doctors, lawyers; a broad range of people to talk about a given subject for about five or ten minutes and then socialise after that. We'd done that for about a year in this second floor room, when we found that Samuel Johnson and Joshua Reynolds held a salon right here in the 1760s, which is amazing. There is a very particular, nice atmosphere about it, though it's sometimes hard to organise when you're busy with other things. It's a really wonderful and rewarding thing to do, and the owner of Black's, Guiseppe Mascoli, is a very good chef; he usually prepares a themed meal to go with it. We usually invite about twenty five people. It's often artists because they tend to be the ones who are prepared to participate at the last minute.

something on those lines. Sometimes through artists as well. One of the things I like about working with artists, you become friends, you help them an later on they help you. Particularly when you work at a development stage, when they're emerging artists. When they get more established they say, I've got a monograph coming up, can you write an essay? Or they'd like to do a show in some country or other, it gets on like that. I feel artists have an affinity with me, like with another artist rather than an academic. I also work with commercial galleries, I can introduce them to artists. It's sometimes easier to do group shows; if you do a solo show with quite a well known artist it

Nomadic Venture

Interview recorded in Edinburgh and London in 2009-10 with Jock McFadyen and Susie Honeyman, in which they discuss exhibitions created in aslternaqtive spaces by The Grey Gallery

The Grey Gallery is an initiative created by the artist Jock McFadyen and musician Susie Honeyman. Staging exhibitions in unusual spaces gives an opportunity to realise some original projects outside of the conventional gallery circuit, and the nomadic Grey Gallery provides a common ground for different disciplines. McFadyen has often worked with writers and musicians; Howard Jacobson has written about his work, as has Will Self, Iain Sinclair and Hugo Williams. The artists Richard Wilson, Helena Ben-Zenou and Bob and Roberta Smith have all participated in Grey Gallery events.

Recorded in Edinburgh 19/08/2009

JMcF It's sort of weaving in and out of music and art. There are Grey Gallery records as well.

SH Yes, at a very embryonic stage. So far we've put out one disc, 'Little Sparta with Sally Timms'. There's a lot of stuff I want to put out, for example, I made a sound track to go with Jock's paintings in 1999. Giles Perring and I made a piece for the A13 exhibition in 2004 and we worked together again on a Jerwood commission in 2005, a piece in response to AnnabelElgar's monumental photographs.

NJ So were these sound tracks to films or solely recorded pieces?

SH The piece I wrote with Giles in 2004 was a sound track for the A13 project. We went out and made field recordings which we worked into a piece we called 'Marsh Music'. We performed it live at the Wapping Project in front of Jock's paintings of the Thames Estuary. Then we made a piece in response to Annabel Elgar's huge photographic works.

JMcF She does photographs as tall as this ceiling. She's a wonderful artist.

Cv/VAR Was this in the context of the A13?

SH No, that was the next year.

JMcF This was another show at Wapping.

SH 'Black Flag' was Annabel's exhibition at Wapping and Jules Wright and the Jerwood Foundation commissioned four musical duos to respond to these photographs. Giles and I were one of the duos. The actual photographs were quite disturbing and we couldn't work out what the narrative was. Annabel was secretive, she wouldn't tell us anything about the images and so we started being quite forensic about them; put them up on a computer screen. In one of the photographs there was a derelict building with an ancient sign. We blew it up and up until we could decipher a place name. Then Giles and I took some recording equipment in a camper van, and tried to find all the locations for the photographs. We pieced together this kind of very loose narrative, and we realised Annabel had been brought up in an army base like Aldershot. We visited all these locations, even using an ordinance survey map to locate the right kind of forest – a pine forest – for one of the photographs. We recorded our music at these locations and used the recordings in the live performance.

So she was dropping clues in her images and then it was up to you.

SH Yes. The other duos simply played in front of the photographs with improvisations, but we'd followed a forensic process.

JMcF Some people did their own thing, but Giles and Susie were the only people to integrate with the work.

SH I can't remember why, but we happened to have this recording from 1890 of Trumpeter Landfrey who sounded the bugle at the Charge of the Light Brigade in 1854. We used the bugle, which can only play notes from the harmonic series – and which fitted in with the proximity of the locations to the army barracks – as a starting point for the notated bits of music and gave a tonal structure to the piece. We also used the Landfrey fragment in the live performance – nobody needed to have known what it was, it was just that bit of a faint and far away clue but it's what actually holds the piece together. That's a piece we did I'd like to put out.

JMcF To go back to the Grey Gallery, its beginnings. The A13 exhibition was curated by The Architecture Foundation with Rowan Moore. There's some sort of parallel here, because I worked with the writer Iain Sinclair. The phrase psychogeography has been applied to his writing about the Estuary, the M25 and that area. A few people some years ago said, 'You know your paintings and his books – you share a subject.' It became apparent we were working in different media but with the same material. One thing we had in common was the A13, the road, and we decided at some point that it would be interesting to collaborate. The road goes from Aldgate Pump, just outside the Roman perimeter of the city and on all the way to Southend. The shortest route from London to the sea. The A13 show at the beautifully distressed Wapping Project was the first time I had ever presented my large paintings, the big empty landscapes, in a venue which was not a gallery; for me it was a revelation to show in this cavernous industrial space. And there were other artists. As well as Iain Sinclair's found objects and storyboards there was an installation from the filmmaker Chris Petit and a large group of monumental works from Helena Ben-Zenou. There was a section of architectural models from a number of people including Tom de Paor and Antony Gormley as well as a filmed interview

Jock McFadyen and Horseshoe Jake in front of McFadyen's painting **'Popular Enclosure'**,
Jake's former place of employment. Courtesy of The Grey Gallery

with Rowan Moore tied on to the back of a lorry as it was being driven down the A13... and there was Susie and Giles' music. My paintings were projected about two or three feet from the wall.

How did you prevent visitors going behind the canvas?

JMcF They couldn't, it was only floated out so far but the real change for me was the realisation that the neutrality aspired to by the conventional white space is false. Sensory deprivation is not possible and the usual white cube insinuates itself just as much as a noisy space.

The galleries being exhibition containers?

JMcF Yes, that's the ethos I guess. The unobtrusive contemporary gallery site intrudes just as much as the chintz of the old hessian walls and gold frames, or the tables and chairs you find in the Fine Art Society in Bond Street.

Having the paintings floating off the wall felt to me more like being in a cinema, when they put the lights out and point everyone the same way, so the suspense is greater. You're there, which is the quality all galleries are looking for. I thought it was the most successful show I'd done since my degree show at Chelsea in the '70s. This was in 2004. My previous exhibition had been at this white cube created at Agnew's in Bond Street. I had a history of showing in galleries, occasionally in museums or the usual venues contemporary painters find themselves in, so Wapping was a new thing for me and it was on a large scale. The Wapping Project is a massive distressed void and it has had a history of exciting shows – the 9/11 Exhibition or Richard Wilson's 'Butterfly'; a crushed up aeroplane being unpicked and put back together by a team of worker ants in orange overalls. It's a serious and a difficult space, because you have to make the show work with the building.

Inspired by Wapping we hired a factory space for the 2005 Edinburgh Festival and got sponsorship from the Scottish Gallery. We made a new exhibition, Road Works, another presentation of my conventional paintings in a non-gallery space. Then we did a London version of Road Works in Bethnal Green. We hired a mirrored car showroom from Rude Wercs in Cambridge Heath Road. (Rude Wercs used to be called Rude Mercs but Mercedes Benz objected to the use of their name and they had to turn the 'M' upside down so they became Rude Wercs.) We called the show 'Road Works at Rude Wercs'. We mounted my paintings on the mirrored walls, it was a risk but the effect certainly amazed me!

It was out of this we decided to create this entity called the Grey Gallery. It was so exciting to work outside of the usual art treadmill. Your dealer puts on a show every two years, you do two mixed exhibitions a year (summer and winter), you put aside work for the art fairs, etc., that routine. After the Wapping experience

our first excursion had been in the Edinburgh Festival. It was quite a success in terms of reviews but we made no money. When we did the 'Rude Wercs' show at Bethnal Green later in the year we had no reviews but made rather a lot of money.

We'd done the factory space in 2005 at Edinburgh, then the 2006 mirrored show in London, and thought, right, now we want to be in the official Edinburgh Festival. We were told, 'You can't be in it unless you're a proper gallery.' So we created a nomadic gallery, The Grey Gallery.

You were open to working with different disciplines in your exhibitions; what kind of experience had you of cooperating with writers?
JMcF When Peter Fuller created Modern Painters, one of the planks of their editorial policy which I thought was very interesting, was to ask authors to write about art. Fuller got Julian Barnes, Howard Jacobson and Peter Jenkins among others to contribute to the magazine. Howard Jacobson wrote about my work in 1991, and Will Self wrote the catalogue for the show Urbasuburba which I made with Humphrey Ocean in 1996 as well as a piece 'There's no reggae in Orkney' for my show at the Pier Art Centre in 1999. Susie subsequently turned this little story into a song for voice, violin and synthesizer. Working across disciplines is something which has always interested me. I have always felt closer to writers, musicians and filmmakers than to other painters so all this made sense to me and The Grey Gallery is an opportunity to push out and find what is possible. After all, no dealer or curator is going to do this for

you on a continual basis. Perhaps every painter should have their own gallery...
Susie, you are with the Mekons?
SH Yes, since 1983, though the band's been going since 1977, it was a Leeds art school band.
And you joined as a violinist?
SH Yes. It's quite a big band, an eight piece band and geographically challenged; four members live in America, four in England. We always did a lot of touring in America. Four members married and ended up living there. America's got a very different attitude to more mature artists. They've got Rolling Stone, Artforum, they've got a critical press we don't have. Longevity isn't seen as doing any harm in the States. We have a small but dedicated fan-base there.
How do you make the music?
SH It's a very natural process, we write songs collectively, together in a room. We tend to hole up somewhere in the country with no distractions and write together over a few days.
You don't trawl studios to find artists for Grey Gallery projects?
SH No, we only show people we know and like.
JMcF It's like gardening, we don't struggle with it, it just suggests itself.

For the Artist

Interview with gallery owner Poppy Sebire recorded at Tate Modern, May 2010

Cv/VAR Let's start with Georgie Hopton's show. How did you get together and leading from that, how do you find your artists?

PS Georgie and I met six or seven years ago when I was working for another gallery, Danielle Arnaud, who is a French dealer based in Lambeth. Georgie had been in a couple of group shows that Danielle had organised and various other shows around London. Our paths kept crossing, and she was one of the artists I was always totally bowled over by. So it was with great pleasure that six years later I came to represent her, and I'm now her representative in London and nationally. She's just opened her exhibition in our temporary exhibition space, the old Chelsea sorting office, at 232 King's Road. In terms of who I work with, it's quite important it's the right relationship.

Like boy and girlfriend you're heavily interdependent and do everything for each other. I commit to my artists in a way that's serious. I take my time about decisions, so they have to be the right person. It's firstly about the work, but then also about how we get along. It can be a very intense relationship but one that I cherish. Georgie trained as a sculptor at Central St.Martin's but she puts her subject under scrutiny from many angles through any medium that might make sense. The recent show 'Cut and Come Again' is made up of photographs of herself alongside her garden produce, bronze casts of the vegetables and plants as well as vegetable prints that are made using the vegetables that she grew in the garden. This multi-disciplinary approach has opened up a conversation in her work that expresses the relationships between one medium and another. A strong sense of herself as tool is another undercurrent that is forever present in her work.

You represent artists but don't actually run a fixed place gallery. You do have a relationship with several galleries here and abroad?

I would describe my artists as international. They're mid-career and to date have had good exposure abroad. I'm trying to generate relationships for them with foreign galleries, so ideally they'd have representatives in other parts of the world. I collaborate with an Italian gallerist for Danny Rolph, Roberto Annichiarico of AR Contemporary, Milan, with an American Gallery, Bravin Lee Programs for Boo Ritson's work, and Georgie Hopton is about to have an exhibition with Brancolini Grimaldi in Rome; so there are lots of other galleries I am in touch with on a weekly basis. We try to put on a solo show for each of our artists once every two years, depending on what they're doing elsewhere. Shows are planned in a way that allows them enough time to develop new work at the right pace. We aim for serious, really well presented exhibitions that best reflect the artist's concerns. The exhibitions are in temporary spaces, which is in response to what is happening in the economy at the moment. I was working

Poppy Sebire in front of **Lloyd George**, 2009, Mixed media on Triplewall by Danny Rolph.
www.poppysebire.com

with the David Risley Gallery for about five years, and as director I helped to build up the gallery in the East End of London. There was a growth in the market and then in 2008 it came tumbling down. I left the gallery in July 2008 with the idea that I was going to open my own space, a fixed premises to build up the gallery home. Of course once the bottom had fallen out of the market; the security of sales vanished and the buyers had gone quiet. There was a knock on effect where nobody was buying, or people who were considering buying pulled back as well. As a result of the recession there were a lot of properties available in London. I am having conversations with plenty of property agents and gallerist friends about which premises to commit to and where. The scene has definitely moved from deepest darkest Hackney back into the West End. The trend was to come back into town and, or course to do that, you need a lot of money.

The commercial property market didn't actually drop its rents.

No. The advantage for me was the West End landlords were having to pay empty rates on all their retail spaces. With a bit of help from my property contacts I came up with the idea to take on central London premises temporarily for an exhibition. The advantages are two fold. My occupancy, albeit temporary, brings life to empty spaces and allows rates relief and I get my space for free in space for free in central London. So two weeks before a show we would be given the keys and we would start to make the space look brilliant, make it look like a gallery.

Do you have to do a lot of work to get it up to scratch?

It depends what property we get. We want to make it look like a proper exhibition space, so that may mean putting a skin within it, redecorating, adding lighting. We need to get the space looking the best we possibly can in order to justify doing it, and to deliver the best possible option for the artist.

And your audiences, are they flexible enough to follow you?

They do follow me and I work incredibly hard to make sure everybody knows where we are. If there's enough energy behind it   I can get everything to happen. I work hard on PR, on securing sales. We go in for two months, work hard on the show; then we might have a gap of a month or so to prepare for the next one.

They're not back to back shows so we have time to take stock and to really focus on each exhibition and each event to do them justice. We'll probably do four or five shows a year and there is an excitement in operating the nomadic space. Everyone is waiting to see where we go next. There is an intrigue that might encourage people to come back to me, wherever it may be.

You seem to have established your identity. What about access to the work, do you arrange studio visits, make introductions that

way? You do need some continuity.

We have a lot of viewable work in each space. We schedule studio visits with the artists who are all happy to oblige to make things happen. I put the work in front of buyers. I encourage people to book an appointment, but if people drop in to get an introduction to what we do and who we show I've got plenty of portfolios to introduce an artist. For me, it's about the initial contact and what you can make happen from that point.

You did Volta in New York, what was your experience there?

We went over for five days, we did a Danny Rolph solo booth and we met a lot of special collectors, as well as people we knew already. It is incredibly important for me to engage with the international scene, especially in New York; to keep having those conversations in person. We'll do select American and European art fairs which are the right fit, the right context for our artists. Everybody is looking at the bigger picture beyond London; everybody goes to these art fairs - America to Europe and vice versa, and it's incredibly important to stay engaged on that level. That's where most of my experience has been: the international and commercial side.

What do you think drives you? What do you get from this activity?

I'm doing it all really for the   artists I work with. I get a huge amount of enjoyment from my relationships with them and their work which I don't want to be exclusive – I want to share it with everybody. There is an incredible buzz around starting from scratch and making something happen. There is a lot of positivity in what we do; the work itself is so rewarding, then finding homes for pieces, the excitement of exhibitions, the very colourful people that we all meet along the way. And I want to make things happen for us and for the gallery to grow to a level where it pushes them to a higher platform.

*Poppy Sebire has now opened a permanent
exhibition space at All Hallows Hall,
6 Copperfield Street, London SE1 0EP.
T: 020 7928 3096
www.poppysebire.com*

Interpreter

*Interview recorded with Edward
Lucie-Smith, 11th July 2011*

*Cv/VAR I mentioned visiting Jacob Epstein's
house in Hyde Park Gate in 1957 with my
parents, to play with Lucian Freud's daughters.
Have you a recollection of Jacob Epstein and
your early experience of the London art
world?*

ELS In 1947-49 I lived in Sydney Street in
Chelsea. That was before the King's Road
became known as the parade ground of
the smart and hip. We lived at the top
end and at the bottom there was a little
shop; and the little shop belonged to a
large bearded man, called KJ Hewett,
who was the dominant antiquities and
tribal art dealer of his time. He was also
one of the people who sold early Bacon
paintings to the Sainsburys in fact.
The great sculptor Epstein was one of his
clients, and used to pop in to see what
was new in tribal art. I used to run
errands for Hewett because I was
fascinated by all that material. I was a
fourteen year old lad running in and out
of the shop. And so I met all these
people: the Squires (he was a dentist who
was a major collector of Old Master
drawings), Bob and Lisa Sainsbury,
Epstein and so forth. My interest in the
visual arts really began with archaeology,
and this helped to feed it.

I was born in Jamaica, I grew up there
until I was thirteen. My father was a civil
servant, but unusually for a civil servant,
belonged to an old West Indian family.
My father's forbears, I believe, had lived

in the West Indies since 1627. There were
no museums, and I was fascinated by
archaeology. I read and re-read Howard
Carter's description of his discovery of the
Tomb of Tutankhamen, which I found in
the Institute of Jamaica library; and of
course when I came to England there
were museums. I went to school
in Canterbury, which had scholarships
for the sons of colonial administrators.
I became a King's Scholar. I was one of
those children who regarded examina-
tions as fun; that is, it was a kind of
eventing. You mounted a little pony,
went along and you leapt over the barrier
and kicked up your heels, so to speak.
Exams never terrified me at that particular stage.

I won a major scholarship to Oxford
when I was just over seventeen, to read
History. I think it was very sensible,
rather than reading English, though I
already had ambitions to be a writer –
I was under a lot of pressure from
Merton, which offered me the scholarship, to read History anyway, because
that was the way my favourite tutor was
thinking.

I then had the choice of doing university
before or after National Service. I opted
for after, because if I arrived in the RAF
with a degree, I got to be an educationalist and would be given a commission.
I was substantially younger than most of
my contemporaries at Oxford, who were
people such as Michael Heseltine, that
generation. They mostly did their
National Service before coming up. They
didn't go to museums. Everybody was
very preoccupied with literature, all the

aspiring poets – Geoffrey Hill, Anthony Thwaite, who were a bit older than me. When I aspired to write about literature for university magazines the editors said "Oh no, no, we've already got people to do that." By implication, people who were much more grown up. But then they said. "Oh, you go to museums, don't you?" People of their sort didn't. I said, "Yes I go to museums, because of the archaeology." So they said, "Oh well then, you can write about art." That's how it started.

I left Oxford, did my National Service, which I actually liked better than Oxford, because I felt I was doing some good – couldn't think what I was doing at Oxford. I emerged and left the RAF on a Friday and started at an advertising agency on a Monday. My family circumstances required I had a job, and I started as a trainee copywriter. The advertising agency I joined was a little nest of poets; Peter Redgrove, Peter Porter, Oliver Bernard – the least known of the Bernard brothers. There was also Trevor Bell, now celebrated as William Trevor, who used to lock himself in the downstairs men's lavatory, writing his short stories.

At that point I used to go to the Portobello Road every Saturday, with a gang of friends. Some of the things I bought there I wish I still had. One of these friends, who's still alive, was a young Swedish dealer called Sven Gahlin. He came to me one day and said, "Dr Gainsborough won't let me stop writing for him." This was in the early days of Art Review. It doesn't happen nowadays, but then Art Review covered practically every gallery. They reviewed practically every exhibition, at least in capsule form. Sven said to me, "You're going to be much better at this than I am. Why don't you do it?" So I started sneaking out of the office, doing reviews for £2 a time and I built up a bit of a track record. I can't remember the order in which these things happened, but I became a deputy to David Sylvester, on The New Statesman; because David was always late on copy.

Eventually one of my friends from Oxford, who had become a BBC radio producer, rang me up and said, "Well we couldn't use you before, because you had no track record. But would you like to try out for The Critics?" I said, "What?" "Oh," he said," you know - The Critics." It was the famous discussion programme. So I trotted along, did my stuff, and it turned out I was fluent. We had to do a book, a film, a play etc. I caught the tail end of the grandees: Stephen Potter, Marghanita Laski.

For some reason, I wasn't particularly put down by them; I was like a little dog going 'yap, yap'! (Laughter). Radio, of course, was much more important then, than it is now. I became a known voice. I even had the experience of people turning round when we were standing in queues, and saying. "You're Edward Lucie-Smith, aren't you?" "How did you know?" "It was the voice." I had people writing to me from linguistic institutes in Scandinavia saying, "We use The Critics as a measure of the pronunciation of standard English; there's something about your voice - where do you come from?" I wrote back to say, "I don't have a West Indian accent, but I probably have a West Indian intonation – rhythm, and that's what's probably bothering you." So it went on; I deputised for John Russell on The Sunday Times. When he went I did not get the job of the Sunday Times art critic, which would certainly have changed my life if I had. Instead of that I started writing art books: the first of which was 'Movements in Art since 1945.' Which has been my calling card ever since.

Was this published by Phaidon?

No, this was Thames & Hudson, in the World of Art series. It came out in 1969, it's still in print. But, with art books, everybody thinks they know better than you. The last edition was overseen by the late Nikos Stangos, who presented me with a list of things he wanted me to do. I looked at him and said, "Nikos, I can't do this, it won't work." "Oh well then.."

We entered upon a long negotiation about what I was prepared to do. I thought, after a struggle, we'd reached an agreement. Nikos retired into hospital for a back operation. The line editor rang me up and said "I am editing the book from the manuscript and Nikos said you would do the following." She read me the list. I replied, "That is not what I said I'd do, it's what I said I wouldn't do." "Oh well, what shall we do then?" "I said "Look, the book is my copyright. I know you have a printer booked for it. We're going to do what I say." So we did." (Laughter)

I remember '60s art books being very weighty.

Well the art book is a dying species, and I may say the big general art book, in which I was one of the experts, I dare to say it, soon won't exist, because it is better done on the web. Except that people don't trust the web as much as they trusted books: rightly or wrongly. A lot of the academic publishers, like Yale, won't accept web references. I ran into that once, when I had to do a job for Yale in a hurry, for a little catalogue. The references were from the web and there was a great fandango about this.

It's a curious time now, because people like to hold art books, but they've lost the ability to read; they have a very low attention threshold.

I've been thinking and saying a lot about this recently. The art world is, in my view, at the moment, very arthritic: it's stiff in the joints. And it's stiff in the joints because it is changing from the old, elitist, top down situation, to a totally different situation, which exists exactly because of the web. The big institutions are burdened with committees, they're not quick enough, in my view, to react. Many people would respond, this is an insolent thing to say. But it is my view, they are absolutely not up to the task, and that means somebody else has got to do it. If you understand the web, and you understand the art world, and you're prepared to do quite a lot of things for no money, then yes, you can do it.

If you take my very recent activities: I did the keynote speech at a conference on feminist art in Lisbon. That was linked to my long time association with the artist Judy Chicago. She's an old friend who I met in New Mexico. I said to Judy years ago, "Why is there no book about you, you're such an important figure."

She replied," Oh, nobody's been able to get one together." I said, "If I got one together, would you do it with me?" "Oh well I suppose I would." It took me about five years to get the spec I wanted. Anyway we did the book, which was the first Judy Chicago career monograph. I think I said one important thing in it: which is that Judy is a characteristically American artist. She's very like artists such as Thomas Hart Benton. That is, people who aim to address a broad audience, who undertake ambitious enterprises without princely patronage.

And they are storytellers?

That sort of thing. Somehow that book changed the perception of Judy. It gave her a place not only in the story of feminism, but in the story of American art. Judy doesn't always like it now when I say I did this for her, but nevertheless, it's the kind of thing that in general I try to do – change an established situation, turn things round a bit. I remember, when I finally got the contract for the book, I got cold feet. I asked Judy, "What's the sisterhood going to say when they discover your monograph has been written by a white European male critic?" She looked me up and down for a long moment, and then she said, "Well, they had their chance." (Laughter) We're still very good friends.

You showed me a Francis Bacon drawing. Did you know him?

I knew Francis, but I never liked him. I was immune to the so-called Francis magic. I used to meet him occasionally at the Gimpels. Endeavouring to make some kind of social bridge, I would mention some person we might have in common and was always rewarded with a put down. He always said something nasty about them. When that had happened three or four times I thought, go away, nasty old queen. Cristiano Lovatelli Ravarino, who gave me the drawing, was an Italian connection of Francis's, best described as a not quite boyfriend. Cristiano remains enraptured to this day. His friendship with Francis was the guiding event to his life. He can't understand why I have definite reservations about Francis's character, which of course extends to reservations about Francis as an artist. That is, I think he's an important artist, but I don't think he's the kind of artist a lot of people think he is.

I saw a big Francis Bacon show at the Hayward in 1998, I came away dissatisfied. The early paintings from the 1950s, were terrific, startling, but then later on, I think he imitated his own tune.

Well that's quite true but, the Bacon drawing you're looking at, belongs to the 1980s. It's a recapitulation of the studies of the Popes and that kind of thing. And the drawing behind you – the Crucifixion, which comes from the same group of is exactly the same thing. I've always believed them to be genuine, but I've always said, that is only my opinion.

The art world is Byzantine: full of assertions, implications and walls of silence.

You know what it's like - the Church. It's much more like religion than anything rational. But listen, in the end what it boils down to with Bacon drawings is the accumulated evidence that, despite all his public denials, he drew a great deal. An enormous amount of graphic stuff - most of it not very good - came out of the studio after he died. Some of the Bacon drawings were found tramped into the floor, when the Dublin City Gallery dismantled the studio to transport it to Ireland. What more do you want as evidence that he actually did draw, even if not very well? If it's a matter of people's belief, or their religion, that Bacon didn't draw, this counts for far more than any argument. Indeed, it counts for more than the actual physical evidence.

Let's get back to a view of art now. A recent article of your was concerned with scale in modernism; it suggested the word 'gigantism' to me. Maybe with the world changing so fast, gigantic works, for example by Richard Serra, may be becoming redundant.

Well just think of it in economic terms, and I'm afraid this may happen. I have been to Bilbao, but only before the building went up, and I have never seen the famous Frank Gehry Guggenheim, but I did actually talk to Gehry in Los Angeles, and saw the model of the new museum. That museum was built for two things: one is was to serve as a shrine to that huge sculpture by Serra, and the other was to act a transatlantic tribute to Frank Lloyd Wright's original Guggenheim in New York. It is just as impractical, I may say, as Lloyd Wright's own version.

It envisages all contemporary art as being like the American art of the late Modernist period. Well art isn't like that anymore. The Guggenheim Bilbao, as far as I know, has a big central room, which is occupied by the Richard Serra you mentioned; the big Serra Snake, and won't accommodate anything else. You have to ask yourself whether this isn't a particular moment in art, frozen in time. And whether museums ought not, in fact, to be more flexible, more adaptable to different things. I had cause to think of this, because I recently wrote a catalogue for a Basque painter called Jesus Mari Lazkano. He was having a show in the other big modern museum in Bilbao, made by two Spanish architects, inspired not by Wright but by Mies van der Rohe. Lazkano is a very skilful realist painter, and he tells it like it is.

Guess what you get in that set of paintings, all inspired by the place where they were going to be shown? Lots of glass, but no walls to hang things on; and a lot of raking light, which is extremely bad for pictures. It picks up every imperfection without enabling you to see the whole composition. The paintings were wonderful of their sort, but also a condemnation of their setting.

There's a peculiar attitude that runs through curator structures towards the visiting public - in Britain particularly - of presenting art they think may be good for you.

There are several questions to pick up here. One is that, while Vasari in the Renaissance, may have believed that art progressed, became more capable of doing x, y and z, his benchmark was how well it represented external reality. Well that standard has long ago disappeared. So art changes, and particularly in a modern society, lives on change, but you can't prove that these changes are an improvement. They're just a necessary function, to keep things going. That's the dominated, elitist, etc.,etc.,etc. It's very arguable whether the idea of an avant garde applies at all.

And now?

The situation is like a reversion to the 19th century, when the big official salons were also dominated by government patronage. There's also an economic pattern. If you look at artistic progression, so-called, it's linked to the economic cycle. That is, after the Eighties, there was a crash. The New Spirit of Painting was suddenly old hat. Then you got a build up in the Nineties, which culminated in Britain with the 'Sensation!' exhibition, arranged by Sir Norman Rosenthal and Charles Saatchi, to fill a sudden gap in the Royal Academy programme. The reason why the exhibition was so immediately successful, was that it was more up to date, due to the emergency situation from which it was born, than such exhibitions usually are.

So after that there was a build up, let us say very loosely, of the reputation of that kind of art, which has been going on ever since. Gradually this has become the preferred art of the establishment. Billionaires now love it. Critics and curators, following the money, are convinced it's the only kind of art worth paying attention to. Yet there's still, inevitably, an impulse towards change. An awful lot of people have an awful lot to lose, if that kind of 1990s art suddenly starts to look flimsy, old fashioned, not quite the thing, not what people are talking about, and so on. There's quite a strong tension at the moment, between defending the citadels of the avant garde

of the Nineties and looking for something new. If you look back a bit further, to the Impressionist Movement, and to impulses repeated throughout the history of Modernism, to the Cubists, to the Surrealists; you'll see that boom-and-bust patterns of that kind have repeated themselves throughout the story of Modernism and Post-Modernism. In the present recession, we are in the most literal sense: due for a change. And it doesn't matter whether you approve of that change, or not. It's going to happen.

Edward Lucie-Smith was born in 1933 at Kingston, Jamaica. He moved to Britain in 1946, and was educated at King's School, Canterbury and Merton College, Oxford, where he read History. Subsequently he was an Education Officer in the R.A.F., then worked in advertising for ten years before becoming a freelance author. He is now an internationally known art critic and historian, who is also a published poet (winner of the John Llewellyn Rhys Memorial Prize), an anthologist and a practicing photographer.

He has published more than a hundred books in all, including a biography of Joan of Arc (recently republished by Penguin in paperback as a 'classic biography'), a historical novel, and more than sixty books about art, chiefly but not exclusively about contemporary work. A number of his art books, among them *Movements in Art since 1945*, Visual Arts of the 20th Century, *A Dictionary of Art Terms* and *Art Today* are used as standard texts throughout the world. Movements in Art since 1945, first published in 1969, has been continuously in print since that date.

He has been curator of a number of exhibitions, including three Peter Moores Projects at the Walker Art Gallery Liverpool, (surveys of contemporary British art), The New British Painting (which toured US venues in 1988-90) and two artist retrospectives, Lin Emery and George Dunbar, both for the New Orleans Museum of Art. He has been a jury member for the John Moores prize exhibition in Liverpool, and for biennials in Cairo, Sharjah, Alexandria and Belgrade. He was curator of 'New British Art'. at the Orion Gallery in Ostend (April-June 2001), of 'New Classicism: Artists of the Ideal', at Palazzo Forti, Verona (April-September 2002), and of 'Gods Becoming Men' at the Frissiras Museum, Athens [July-September 2004). He has recently become the curator of the new Bermondsey Project Space in London S.E.1

Collections Guide

England, Wales
& Scotland

Flank wall of Tate Modern, Bankside
Cv/VAR Archive

CENTRAL LONDON

Apsley House
149 Piccadilly W1
Telephone: 020 7499 5676

Collection of the Duke of Wellington, gathered during his military campaigns: over two hundred paintings, including works by Rubens, Goya, Velázquez.

www. apsleyhouseguide.co.uk

Barbican Centre
Silk Street, EC2
Telephone: 020 7638 4141

Exhibitions of 19th and 20th century art, from van Gogh to contemporary textiles. Examples of the Corporation of London's collection, including paintings by Matthew Smith, are also on display

www. barbican.org.uk/artgallery

Ben Uri Art Society
108A Boundary Road. Off Abbey Road.
St Johns Wood. London NW8 0RH
Telephone: 020 7604 3991.

Collection of Jewish art, including paintings, drawings, prints and sculptures byBomberg, Gertler, Kramer and Epstein.

www. benuri.org.uk

The Bank of England Museum
The Bank of England,
Threadneedle Street, London EC2.
Telephone: 020 7601 5545

Traces the history of The Bank of England from its foundation in 1694 to the present day. Examples of gold ingots, banknotes and the changing face of coinage.

www. bankofengland.co.uk/museum

The British Council Collection
BC Visual Arts Department,
11 Portland Place, W1
Telephone: 020 7389 3060

The British Council holds works in all media and information archives of the range of significant 20th century British artists, which are distributed in its three hundred centres through Europe and the Far East. *Specialist research enquiries only*

www. collection.britishcouncil.org

The British Library
St.Pancras London WC2.
Telephone: 020 7323 7222

Comprehensive resource for research and scholarship. Holds a copy of each publication produced in Britain, from originalmanuscripts of The Magna Carta 1215.

www. bl.uk

The British Museum
Great Russell Street London WC2
Telephone: 020 7636 1555

Comprehensive collection of artefacts of ancient civilizations: from Asia, Rome, Greece, Egypt, Celtic and Anglo-Saxon. Temporary changing exhibitions feature theme studies of specific areas of Western art and antiquity.

www. britishmuseum.org

Carlyle's House
24 Cheyne Row, Chelsea,
London SW3 5HL
Telephone: 020 7352 7087

Queen Anne period town house of Victorian writer and historian Thomas Carlyle from 1834. Portraits of the writer and his wife, with relics and personal mementos of his life and times.

www. nationaltrust.org.uk/main/w-carlyleshouse

Courtauld Gallery
Somerset House,
Strand, WC2
Telephone: 020 7873 2526

Major holding of the Impressionist movement of painters in UK: Manet,van Gogh, Cezanne, Renoir; also the Courtauld Collection of art from the early Renaissance to Goya and other Western masters.

www. courtauld.ac.uk/

Crafts Council
44a Pentonville Road, N1
Telephone: 020 7278 7700

Resource and study centre for crafts design UK. Changing exhibitions, bookshop and slide library.

www. craftscouncil.org.uk

Cuming Museum
155-157 Walworth Road, SE17
Telephone: 020 7701 1342

The personal collection of Richard Cuming and Son, from 1872, including items from archeological digs in Southwark, and the curious Lovat Collection of London Superstitions

www. southwark.gov.uk/cumingmuseum

De Morgan Foundation
30 Vicarage Crescent,
Battersea SW11
Telephone: 020 8788 1341

The paintings and drawings of Evelyn de Morgan (1850-1919), and ceramics by William de Morgan (1839-1917); also works by Spencer Stanhope, Strudwick and Cadogan Cowper.

www. demorgan.org.uk

Design Museum
Butlers Wharf, Shad Thames SE1
Telephone: 020 7403 6933

Survey of commercial and utilitarian design of 20th century: Review Gallery explores range of new products, with study programme changing rota of temporary exhibitions and events.

www. designmuseum.org

Eastbury Manor House
Barking IG11
Telephone: 020 8507 0119

Elizabethan Manor House used by London Borough of Barking and Dagenham as Arts and Cultural Centre.

www. barking-dagenham.gov.uk/4-eastbury

Fenton House
Windmill Hill,
Hampstead NW3
Telephone: 020 7435 3471

Late 17th century house with wide-range of porcelain and early musical instruments.

www. nationaltrust.org.uk/main/w-fentonhouse

Fan Museum
12 Crooms Hill, Greenwich SE10
Telephone: 020 8305 1441

Major collection of 2000 fans, of mainly European origin. Workshops for fan-craft and conservation.

www. fan-museum.org

Freud Museum
20 Maresfield Gardens,
Hampstead NW3 Telephone: 020 7435 2002/5167

Last residence of Sigmund Freud, from 1938. Personal collection of c. 1800 antiquities, from Egypt, Greeece, and the Far East. Library and study in original state. Occasional temporary exhibitions.

www. freud.org.uk

Geffrye Museum
Kingsland Road, Hackney E2

Almshouses built in 1715. Presents a sequence of period room sets from medieval to present day interiors. Collection of relics and curios reflecting changes in fashions and tastes.

www. geffrye-museum.org.uk

The George Inn
The George Inn Yard,
77 Borough High Street,
Southwark SE1
Telephone: 020 7407 2056

Galleried inn preserved from 17th century, mentioned by Charles Dickens in Little Dorritt. Leased as a public house.

www. nationaltrust.org.uk/main/
w-georgeinn

Goldsmiths Hall
Foster Lane EC2
Telephone: 020 7606 7010

The Goldsmiths Company Hall houses collection of plate and jewellery dating from 14th century to present, and display of modern medals.

www. thegoldsmiths.co.uk/hall

Government Art Collection
DCMS 2-4 Cockspur Street
London SW1Y 5DH
Telephone: 020 7580 9120

Amongst the largest holdings of 20th c.British art, collection includes oils, watercolours, prints, sculptures and tapestries. Works may be viewed by appointment.

www.gac.culture.gov.uk/information/

Ham House
Ham, Richmond TW10
Telephone: 020 8940 1950

Collection includes fine furniture, textiles and paintings. Centre of Court life in 1670s, when residence of Duke of Lauderdale. formal gardens.

www.richmond.gov.uk/ham_house

Hampstead Museum
Burgh House, New End Square,
Hampstead NW3
Telephone: 020 7431 0144

Charts the history of Hampstead, with paintings by Helen Allingham, George Richmond, CRW Nevinson and others.

www.burghhouse.org.uk/museum

Hogarth's House
Hogarth Lane, Great
West Road, W4
Telephone: 020 8994 6757
The artist's summer residence from 1749 to 1764. Displays Hogarth's satirical engravings, including The Rake's Progress and The Harlot's Progress.

www.visithounslow.com/Hogarths_House

Horniman Museum
100 London Road, SE23
Telephone: 020 8699 2339

Donated by founder of Hornimans Tea, includes a personal collection of ethnography and natural history; Living Waters Aquarium and New Music Room.
www.horniman.ac.uk

Imperial War Museum
Lambeth Road SE1
Telephone: 020 7416 5000

Permanent collection includes important war-works by Burra, Nash, Gross and Wyndham Lewis. Archive of prints covers 19th/20th century European artists. Changing programme of temporary exhibitions.

www.iwm.org.uk

Institute of Contemporary Arts
Nash House, The Mall SW1
Telephone: 020 7930 3647

Centre for experimental work and installations by international artists. Changing programme of exhibitions, films and conferences.

www.ica.org.uk

Jewish Museum
Raymond Burton House,
129-131 Albert Street NW1
Telephone: 020 7284 7384

History of Jewish life and religion. Collection includes 16th century carved Venetian synagogue ark, illuminated marriage contracts and Byzantine votive plaque.

www.jewishmuseum.org.uk

Dr Johnson's House
17 Gough Square EC4
Telephone: 020 7353 3745

Samuel Johnson's residence from 1748 to 1759, restored its original condition.Contains portraits,books, and original editions of Johnson's Dictionary.

www.drjohnsonshouse.org

Kensington Palace
State Apartments
Kensington W8
Telephone: 0844 482 7777
Interior decorations by Grinling Gibbons and William Kent. Display of Ceremonial Dress Collection; paintings by Rubens, van Dyck, Kneller, Maclise.

www.hrp.org.uk/KensingtonPalace

Kenwood House
Hampstead Lane NW3
Telephone: 020 8348 1286

17th century mansion in own grounds on Hampstead Heath, re-modelled in neo-classical style. Contains the collection of Edward Guinness, First Earl of Iveagh, bequeathed in 1927. Includes Hals, Rembrandt, Vermeer, Reynolds, Turner and Gainsborough.

www. english-heritage.org.uk/daysout/properties/
kenwood-house

Kew Bridge Steam Museum
Green Dragon Lane,
Brentford, W4
Telephone: 020 8568 4757

Display of examples of Victorian engineering: waterworks, and railway steam engines in working order.

www. kbsm.org

Leighton House
12 Holland Park W1
Telephone: 020 7602 3316

Newly restored residence of Frederick, Lord Leighton, President of the Royal Academy (1830-96). Designed in the 'Aesthetic Style' to evoke an Arabic interior. Collection of 16th century Islamic tiles, with further decoration by Crane and De Morgan. Occasional temporary exhibitions.

www. rbkc.gov.uk/LeightonHouse

London Transport Museum
Covent Garden Market WC2
Telephone: 020 7379 6344

The historical development of Londons transport system. Features buses, underground trains and other conveyances, with posters and graphics from each period.

www. ltmuseum.co.uk

MCC Museum
Lords Cricket Ground NW8
Telephone: 020 7289 1611

Artefacts and mementos of the national pastime of Cricket dating from 16th century to the present. Paintings by Hayman, Watts, Orpen, Ward and Toynbee.

www. lords.org/history/mcc-museum

Mall Galleries
The Mall SW1
Telephone: 020 7930 6844

Directed by The Federation of British Artists. Changing rota of Society Exhibitions, with lecture and demonstration programme. Home of the Royal Societies of Portrait Painters and Watercolourists.

www. mallgalleries.org.uk

Museum of London
150 London Wall
London EC2Y 5HN
Telephone: 020 7001 9844

Chronological record of the Capital City from pre-history to the present. Room sets and models with archeological finds. Changing programme of temporary exhibitions.

www. museumoflondon.org.uk

Museum of the Order of St.John
St.John's Gate,
Clerkenwell, EC1
Telephone: 020 7324 4005

Historical collection of The Order of St John (f.c.1099, Jerusalem). Items include: coins, armour, books, manuscripts, jewellery and insignia. Also paintings and prints by Gianni, Galea, Dingli and Zinkeisen.

www. sja.org.uk/museum

Musical Museum
368 High Street Brentford W4
Telephone: 020 8560 8108

Working automatic musical instruments from musical boxes to great Wurlitzer theatre organ. Early recordings in the collection.

www. musicalmuseum.co.uk

National Army Museum
Royal Hospital Road, Chelsea SW3
Telephone: 020 7881 2455

The British Army from fomation of Yeoman Guard (1485) to present day. Display of medals, uniforms, weapons and memorabilia. Programme of special exhibitions.

www. national-army-museum.ac.uk

The National Gallery
Trafalgar Square WC2
Telephone: 020 7747 2423

Founded in 1824 to display collection of 38 paintings by Western Masters, from collection of John Julius Angerstein, now holds in excess of 2,200 works of art from 13th to 20th century. Major works by Masaccio, Piero Della Francesca, Titian, Rembrandt, Velázquez, Goya, Turner, Constable , Cézanne and van Gogh. Changing rota of special exhibitions, lecture and educational programme.

www. nationalgallery.org.uk

The National Portrait Gallery
St.Martin's Place WC2
Telephone: 020 7306 0055

Major collection of portrait, private and public, from Tudor Schools to 20th century examples. Works in all media. Changing programme of themed exhibitions.

www. npg.org.uk/

National Touring Exhibitions of Arts Council Collection
South Bank Centre, Royal Festival Hall London SE1
Telephone: 020 7921 0600

Collection of The Arts Council of Great Britain of over 7000 works representing c.2000 British artists. Works are included in special touring exhibitions disseminated throughout UK.

www. artscouncil.org.uk

Osterley Park
Isleworth, Middlesex TW7
Telephone: 020 8232 5050

Set in landscaped park with lakes, Osterley was built in 1575 for founder of the Royal Exchange, Sir Thomas Gresham. Transformed in 18th century to a neo-classical villa, decorated by Robert Adam.

www. osterleypark.org.uk

The Percival David Foundation of Chinese Art
53 Gordon Square WC1
Telephone: 020 7387 3909

c.1700 pieces of Chinese ceramics ranging from Sung, Yuan, Ming and Qing Dynasties.Lecture programme & research archive. Limited access.
www. soas.ac.uk

Pitshanger Manor Museum
Mattock Lane, Ealing W5
Telephone: 020 8567 1227

Former country villa of architect Sir John Soane, redesigned by him1800-04. Holds collection of Martinware pottery made between 1877 and 1914. Changing exhibitions of historical and contemporary art.

Queen's Gallery
Buckingham Palace SW1
Telephone: 020 7799 2331

The Royal Collection of Art, from Leonardo and Michelangelo to George Stubbs and Thomas Gainsborough. Themed displays present changing selections from the extensive holdings.

www. queensgallery.co.uk

Ranger's House
Chesterfield Walk,
Blackheath SE10
Telephone: 020 8853 0035

Contains Dolmetsch collection of musical instruments (loaned from Horniman Museum), 17th and 18th century portraits by Larkin, Kneller and Hogarth

www. english-heritage.org.uk/
rangers-house

Royal Academy of Arts
Burlington House,
Piccadilly W1J 0BD
Telephone: 020 7300 8000

Founded in 1768 as a society of artists by Sir Joshua Reynolds, the RA functions as a school of art, exhibition space and archive of rarely displayed Diploma Works. A quarterly cycle of exhibitions centres around major historical and themes, with an annual summer show of amateur and professional British artists.

www.royalacademy.org.uk

Zabludowicz Collection
176 Prince of Wales Road
London NW5 3PT
Telephone: 020 7428 8940

Inaugarated in 2007 by collectors Anita and Poju Zabludowicz the centre provides a forum for innovative work, presented in a changing programme of exhibitions, talks and seminars.

www.**zabludowicz**collection.com

Royal Institute of British Architects:
The Drawings Collection
Victoria and Albert Museum
Cromwell Road
London, SW7 2RL
Telephone: 020 7307 3708

The archive of plan drawings was begun in 1834, and now extends to over 500,000 items from 1480 to the present day. The collection includes models, drawings, instruments and portraits of architects.

www.architecture.com/
Library**Drawings**AndPhotographs

Saatchi Gallery
Duke of Yorks HQ
Kings Road, London SW3 4SQ
Telephone: 020 7823 2363

Major holding of international contemporary art with emphasis on worldwide view. Permanent installation: 20:50 by Richard Wilson.

www.saatchi-gallery.co.uk

Sir John Soane's Museum
13 Lincoln's Inn FieldsWC2
Telephone: 020 7405 2107

Built by Sir John Soane in 1812-1813 as a private residence. Contains his collection of art and antiquities ranging from an Egyptian sarcophagus to works by Canaletto and Piranesi. Research library open by appointment.

www.soane.org

Spitalfields Heritage Centre
19 Princelet Street, Spitalfields E1
Telephone: 020 7247 5352

A mid-18th century building which housed immigrant family of Hugenot silk weavers. Used more recently to teach English to Bengali women working in the East End garment industry.

www.spitalfields.org.uk/museums

The Strang Print Room
University College London,
Gower Street WC1
Telephone: 020 7679 2540

Holding of 800 drawings and casts by neo-classical sculptor John Flaxman, as well as major collection of 16th to 18th century European drawings and prints.

www.ucl.ac.uk/museums/uclart

Sutton House
2 & 4 Homerton High Street E9
Telephone: 020 8986 2264
Tudor red-brick house built in 1535 by Sir Rafe Sadleir, Secretary of State to Henry VIII. Includes wall paintings.

www.nationaltrust.org.uk/main/
w-suttonhouse

Tate Britain
Millbank SW1
Telephone: 020 7887 8888

Established by sugar magnate Sir Henry Tate, the Tate Gallery houses the major holding of British and European modern art in UK. The collection is multi-stranded with historical works from Tudor times to 19th century artists, Constable to Millais. Tate Britain features restrospectives of modern British artists where Tate Modern focuses on international developments.

www.tate.org.uk

Tate Modern
Bankside SE1
Telephone: 020 7887 8888

Opened in May 2000 Tate Modern houses the Tate Galleries collection of contemporary art and examples drawn from 19th and beyond of modernist and vanguard artists. The displays arranged in upper floor galleries of the converted power station have an emphasis on Surrealism and international modernism. The massive Turbine Hall makes a dramatic context for specially commissioned installations, sculptures and experiential environments.

www.tate.org.uk

Thomas Coram Foundation
49 Mecklenburgh Square
London WC1N 2NY
Telephone: 020 7520 0385

Paintings by Hogarth decorate the Governor's Court Room of old Foundling Hospital. Also holds range of musical scores by Handel, funiture and other mementos of the institution,

www.thomascoram.camden.sch.uk

Victoria & Albert Museum
Cromwell Road SW7
Telephone: 020 7942 2000

The national centre for art and design, holds sculpture, ceramics, glass, fashion and other branches of craftwork. Major archive of photography, library and changing exhibitions programme.

www.vam.ac.uk

The Wallace Collection
Hertford House, Manchester Square W1
Telephone: 020 7563 9500

The collection of 4th Marquess of Hertford (1800-70), includes paintings, furniture, clocks, porcelain and arms and armour. Works by Boucher, Watteau, Rembrandt, Hals, Van Dyck, and the 18th century English School.

www.wallacecollection.org

2 Willow Road
2 Willow Rd, Hampstead NW3
Telephone: 020 7435 6166

Designed by architect Erno Goldfinger in 1939, and his home to 1987. Modernist building includes art and artefacts from Moore to Ernst.

www.nationaltrust.org.uk/2willowroad/
w-2willowroad-goldfinger

William Morris Gallery
Lloyd Park Lodge, Forest Road,
Walthamstow E17
Telephone: 020 8527 3782

Occupied by the Morris family from1848 to 1856. Gallery opened in 1950, to house and present the work of William Morris, designer, socialist and poet. Examples of textiles, wallpaper and stained glass work.

www.walthamforest.gov.uk/
william-morris

Woodlands Art Gallery
90 Mycenae Road, Blackheath SE3
Telephone: 020 8858 5847

Built in 1774 as summer residence of John Julius Angerstein, philanthropic collector and source of the first National Gallery. No permanent collection, but centre for changing exhibitions of contemporary art.

www. milesfaster.co.uk/london/**woodlands-art-gallery**

GREATER LONDON AREA

Chiswick House
Burlington Lane, Chiswick W4
Telephone: 020 8995 0508

Designed by Richard Boyle, Third Earl of Burlington in neo-Palladian manner, and built 1725-29.Contains small collection of 18th century portraits. Formal Gardens. English Heritage Property (EH)

*www. www.english-heritage.org.uk/daysout/properties/
chiswick-house/*

Gunnersbury Park Musem
Gunnersbury Park W3
Telephone: 020 8992 1612

Collection of coaches and utilitarian implements from Victorian era, with items of local interest.

www.gunnersburyfriends.org/

Marble Hill House
Richmond Road,
Twickenham, Middlesex
Telephone: 020 8892 5115

Neo-Palladian villa, built 1723-29 for Henrietta Howard, Countess of Suffolk. Holds works by Hogarth, Wilson, Thornhill. Decorative interior.

www.english-heritage.org.uk/daysout/properties/
marble-hill-house

Old Speech Room Gallery
Harrow School, 5 High Street Harrow on the Hill,
Middlesex
Telephone: 020 8872 8021

Collection of antiquities from ancient Egypt, Rome and Greece. Small English art collection and printed ephemera. Occasional exhibitions.

www.culture24.org.uk/se000029

Orleans House Gallery
Riverside, Twickenham, Middlesex
Telephone: 020 8744 0501

Built in 1710, riverside villa contains renowned Octagon room designed by James Gibbs. Gallery presents changing programme of exhibitions of historical interest, and houses the Ionides and Richmond upon Thames art collections, forming a record of the locality.
www.richmond.gov.uk/orleans_house_gallery

Southall Library
Osterley Park Road,
Southall, Middlesex UB2
Telephone: 020 8574 3412

Collection of Martinware salt-glazed Pottery produced between 1877-1914.

www.ealing.gov.uk/services/leisure/libraries/
find_a_library

Syon House
Syon Park, Brentford,
Middlesex TW8
Telephone: 020 8568 0134

Major collection of portraits by van Dyck, Lely, Huysmans, Gainsborough, Reynolds. Robert Adam interior.

www.syonpark.co.uk

SURREY

Clandon Park
West Clandon, Guildford GU4
Telephone: 01483 222502
Built in 1730s for Second Lord Onslow by Giacomo Leoni. Contains family collection of furniture, porcelain and needlework.

www.clandonpark.co.uk

Hampton Court Palace
Hampton Court, East Molesey, Surrey
Telephone: 0844 482 7777

Built for Cardinal Wolsey in 1514, expanded by Henry VIII in 1520s. Extensive collection of Royal Portraits by Holbein, van Leemput, Lely, Honthorst. Tapestries. Significant Triumph of Caesar, major work by Mantegna in Orangery.

www.hrp.org.uk

Hatchlands Park
East Clandon, Guildford, GU4
Telephone: 01483 222482

Interiors by Robert Adam; the Cobbe Collection of keyboard instruments; garden designed by Gertrude Jekyll.

www. nationaltrust.org.uk/main/w-hatchlandspark

Polesden Lacey
Great Bookham, nr
Dorking RH5
Telephone: 01372 458203

Regency villa redesigned after 1906 by Mrs Ronald Greville. Gathering point for the Edwardian Royal Circle. Collection of early medieval to 17th century Dutch paintings, library, ephemera and furniture.

www.nationaltrust.org.uk/polesdenlacey

SUSSEX (East)

Brighton Museum and Art Gallery
Church Street Brighton BN1
Telephone: 03000 290900

Archaeology, ethnography, musical instruments, fine and decorative arts. Range of works from Jan Lievens to the Camden Town Group.

www.brighton.virtualmuseum.info

Charleston
Firle, nr Lewes BN8
Telephone: 01323 811626

Home of Vanessa Bell and Duncan Grant, and centre for The Bloomsbury Group. Contains examples of their creative productions: murals, decorative pottery and textiles.

www.charleston.org.uk

Glynde Place
Glynde nr Lewes BN8
Telephone: 01273 858 224

16th century mansion with holding of works by Kneller, Zoffany, Gainsborough, Rubens.

www.glynde.co.uk/glynde_place

Lamb House
Watchbell Lane Rye TN31
Telephone: 01892 890 110

Home of writer Henry James from 1898-1916, containing mementoes and personal posessions.

www.nationaltrust.org.uk/main/
w-lambhouse

Breon O'Casey **Aphrodite** 2008
53 x 30.5″ Edition of Three. Included in a solo
exhibition of the artist at Somerset House London, October to January 2011.
Photo © Breon O'Casey Courtesy Courtauld Gallery

Monks House
Rodmell, Lewes BN7
Telephone: 01323 870001

House and garden of publisher and author Leonard and Virginia Woolf from 1919.

www. nationaltrust.org.uk/main/w-monkshouse

SUSSEX (West)

Arundel Castle
Arundel BN18
Telephone: 01903 882173

Home of the Duke of Norfolk's dynasty for 700 years. Large collection of family portraits, and works of the English, Dutch and Flemish Schools.

www.arundelcastle.org

Petworth House
Petworth GU28
Telephone 01798 342207

Home of the Earls of Egremont, major patrons and collectors of art. Holds works by Turner, van Dyck, Reynolds and Blake. Set in formal gardens and parkland.

www.nationaltrust.org.uk/…
petworthhouse

The Royal Pavilion
Brighton BN1
Telephone: 03000 290900

Classical villa redesigned by John Nash for The Prince Regent between 1815 and 1822 in oriental style. Fantasy interiors in Chinese style. Rich collection of plate and silver, with decorative art.

www.royalpavilion.org.uk

Cass Sculpture Foundation
Goodwood, nr. Chichester
West Sussex, PO18 0QP
Telephone: 01243 538449

Established in 1992, the Foundation has formed a collectionof eighty large sculpture which are available for loan or purchase.Includes work by Phillip King, Anthony Caro, Michael Kidner, and Anish Kapoor.

www.sculpture.org.uk

Uppark
South Haring, Petersfield GU31
Telephone: 01730 825857

17th century mansion located high in South Downs. Fetherstonehaugh collection of fine and decorative art. Recently restored.

www. nationaltrust.org.uk/main/
w-uppark

Wakehurst Place
Ardingly, nr Haywards Heath RH17
Telephone: 01444 894066

Natural collection of shrubs and trees, extensive themed gardens and nature reserve.

www.kew.org/visit-wakehurst

Worthing Museum and Art Gallery
Chapel Road, Worthing BN11
Telephone: 01903 221 140

Collections of archeology, local history, costume and applied arts. 19th & 20th century watercolours and work by Camden Town Group. Changing temporary exhibitions.

www.worthing.gov.uk › Services ›
Leisure and Culture

THE HOME COUNTIES:
*Bedfordshire, Berkshire, Buckinghamshire,
Cambridgeshire, Hertfordshire*

BEDFORDSHIRE

Bedford Museum
Castle Lane Bedford MK40
Telephone: 01234 353323

www.bedfordmuseum.org

Cecil Higgins Art Gallery and Museum
Castle Close, Bedford MK40
Telephone: 01234 211222

Personal collection by local brewer of ceramics and glass from major factories, and of Bedford lace. Examples of major British artists from Gainsborough to Blake.

www.cecilhigginsartgallery.org/

Luton Hoo
Luton Bedforshire LU1
Telephone: 01582 22955

The Wernher art collection includes art of the Italian Renaissance and Dutch Schools: Lippi, Bermejo, Rembrandt, Metsu, Steen. Holds enamels, bronzes and jewellery, including Fabergé.

www.lutonhooestate.co.uk

Woburn Abbey
Woburn Bedfordshire MK43
Telephone: 0525 290666

Collection includes works by Rembrandt, Claude, Cuyp, Teniers, Velázquez. Antiques centre and shops.

www.woburn.co.uk/abbey

BERKSHIRE

Basildon Park
Lower Basildon, Reading RG8
Telephone: 0118 984 3040

18th century house by John Carr of York, contains paintings, furniture, decorative Shell Room. Formal gardens.

www. nationaltrust.org.uk/main/basildonpark

Stanley Spencer Gallery
King' Hall, High Street,
Cookham SL6
Telephone: 01628 471 885

Devoted to eccentric English visionary Stanley Spencer (1891-1959), with significant paintings held on long-term loan.

www.stanleyspencer.org.uk

Windsor Castle
Windsor Berkshire SL4
Telephone: 020 7766 7304

The Royal Residence since William The Conqueror. Portrait collection includes Lawrence, van Dyck, Holbein, Mytens. Print Room holds Leonardo manuscripts.

www. royalcollection.org.uk/Windsor

BUCKINGHAMSHIRE

Ascott
Wing nr Leighton Buzzard LU7
Telephone: 01296 688242

The Anthony de Rothschild Collection, comprising French and English furniture, oriental porcelain, and paintings.

www. ascottestate.co.uk/

Claydon House
Middle Claydon nr
Buckingham MK18
Telephone: 01296 730349

Highly decorated interior in Chinese and Gothic styles. Relics of the Civil War, and Florence Nightingale museum.

www. nationaltrust.org.uk/main/w-claydonhouse

Cliveden
Taplow, Maidenhead SL6
Telephone: 01628 605069

Home of Nancy , Lady Astor, built in 1851, once society centre and now let as an hotel.
www.nationaltrust.org.uk/main/w-cliveden.

Hughenden Manor
High Wycombe HP14
Telephone: 01494 755 573

Purchased in 1847 by Benjamin Disraeli, who lived there until 1881. Contains mementoes, books, documents of the owner. Access to the Hughenden Estate.

www.nationaltrust.org.uk/main/w-hughendenmanor

Stowe
Buckingham MK18
Telephone: 01280 818280/282

House owned by Stowe School. State rooms may be visited. Large formal gardens.

www.stowe.co.uk

Waddesdon Manor
Waddesdon nr Aylesbury HP18
Telephone: 01296 653 226

Simulates style of French Chateau, built for Rothschild family in 1870s.Collections includes master paintings of English School, S vres porcelain, carpets and furniture.

www.waddesdon.org.uk

West Wycombe Park
West Wycombe HP14
Telephone: 016284 88675

Site of Sir Francis Dashwoods Hellfire Club in 18th century. Italianate design, classical temples, collection of decorate pictures and sculptures.

www.nationaltrust.org.uk/main/w-westwycombepark

CAMBRIDGESHIRE

Anglesey Abbey
Lode Cambridge CB5
Telephone: 01223 810 080

Dates from 1600, and contains the Fairhaven collection of painting and furniture. Extensive gardens.

www.nationaltrust.org.uk/angleseyabbey

Fitzwilliam Museum
Trumpington Street Cambridge CB2
Telephone: 01223 332900

Greek, Roman and Egyptian antiquities, Western and Oriental textiles,illuminated manuscripts, books and coins. Range of art from 17th to 20th century.

www.fitzmuseum.cam.ac.uk

Kettles Yard
Castle Street Cambridge CB3
Telephone: 01223 748 100

Personal collection of Jim and Helen Ede includes estate of Henri Gaudier-Brzeska, oriental artefacts and sundry examples of 30s British abstraction. Changing programme of contemporary exhibitions.

www.kettlesyard.co.uk/

Museum of Classical Archaeology
Sidgwick Site, Sidgwick Avenue,
Cambridge CB3
Telephone: 01223 335151

Plastercasts of classical sculptures from 6th century BC to 2nd century AD. Specialist research centre.

www.classics.cam.ac.uk/museum

HERTFORDSHIRE

Hatfield House
Hatfield AL9
Telephone: 01707 287010

The estate of the Earls of Salibury, built 1610. Portraits from Tudor to present day, strong in Jacobean portraits. Also tapestries, furniture and armour.

www. hatfield-house.co.uk

Henry Moore Foundation
Dane Tree House Perry Green
Herts SG10 6EE
Telephone: 01279 843 333

Founded by the artist in 1977, the Henry Moore Foundation manages the estate and legacy of the artist. It awards grants to arts organisations in the UK and elsewhere.

www.henrymoore.org

Shaw's Corner
Ayot St.Lawrence nr Welwyn AL6
Telephone: 01438 820307

Home of playwright and novelist George Bernard Shaw from 1906-30. Literary and personal relics of the author.

www.nationaltrust.org.uk/main/
w-shawscorner

Wimpole Hall
Arrington, Royston SG8
Telephone: 01223 206000

Collection of Elsie, daughter of Rudyard Kipling, includes paintings by Wotton, Ramsay and Tissot.

www.wimpole.org

KENT

Chartwell
Westerham TN16
Telephone: 01732 866368

Home of Sir Winston Churchill from 1924. Rooms left as in his lifetime. Collection of his views of the gardens and other subjects.

www. nationaltrust.org.uk/main/w-chartwell

Ightham Mote
Ivy Hatch Sevenoaks TN15
Telephone: 01732 810378

Medieval manor house with subsequent additions. Noted ceiling painting c.1520, Jacobean details.

www.nationaltrust.org.uk/main/
w-ighthammote

Knole
Sevenoaks TN15
Telephone: 01732 450608

Owned by Lord Sackville, Knole is the largest private house in England. Thirteen state rooms open to public, contain strong holding of historical portraits, including van Dyck, Kneller and Gainsborough. Also collection of furniture, silverware and Flemish tapestries.

www.nationaltrust.org.uk/knole

Leeds Castle
Maidstone ME17
Telephone: 01622 765400

www.leeds-castle.com

**Maidstone Museum
and Bentlif Art Gallery**
St.Faiths Street Maidstone ME14
Telephone: 01622 602838

Collection of costume, armour, ethnography, archaeology, and paintings by artists of the locality.

www.museum.maidstone.gov.uk

Quebec House
Westerham TN16
Telephone: 01732 868381

Early home of General Wolfe. Documents and memorabilia of Wolfes family history and career. Exhibition set of The Battle of Quebec 1759.

www.nationaltrust.org.uk/main/
w-quebechouse

**The Royal Museum
and Art Gallery**
High Street Canterbury CT1
Telephone: 01227 452 747

Natural history, local archaeology, fine and applied art. Art collection includes examples from Gainsborough to Epstein.

www.canterbury.gov.uk

Sissinghurst
Sissinghurst nr Cranbrook TN17
Telephone: 01580 710701

Gardens created by Vita Sackville-West and Sir Harold Nicolson. Access to study and library in Elizabethan mansion.

www.nationaltrust.org.uk/main/
w-sissinghurstcastlegarden

Smallhythe Place
Smallhythe, Tenterden TN30
Telephone: 01580 762334

The home of the actress Ellen Terry from 1899 to 1928. Retains souvenirs of her life and career. Includes The Barn Theatre and Terrys rose garden.

www.theheritagetrail.co.uk/notable houses/
smallhythe_place

Squerryes Court
Westerham Kent TN16
Telephone: 01959 5622345

Built in 1681 and owned since then by the Warde family. Substantial art collection ranges from Dutch 17th century: of van Goyen and Ruisdael, to family portraits by Dahl, Opie and Kneller.

www. squerryes.co.uk/info

ESSEX

Chelmsford and Essex Regiment Museum
Oaklands Park, Moulsham Street, Chelmsford,
Essex CM2
Telephone: 01245 605700

Features costume, archaeology and local history. Examples of Essex based artists: Bawden and Nash. Also collection of 18th century glassware.

www. friendschelmsmuseums.btik.com

Minories Art Gallery
74 High Street Colchester CO1
Telephone: 01206 712437

20th century Anglian painters, including works by Paul and John Nash. Extensive archives may be viewed by appointment.

www.theminories.co.uk

Paycockes
West Street Coggeshall
Colchester CO6
Telephone: 01376 561305

Merchant's house built c.1500. Ornate panelling and embellished borders. Display of famed Coggeshall lace. Garden.

www.nationaltrust.org.uk/main/
w-paycockes

Sir Alfred Munnings Art Museum
Castle House, Dedham nr Colchester CO7
Telephone: 01206 322127

Celebrated Royal Academician's studies of horses and country life.

www.siralfredmunnings.co.uk

University of Essex Gallery
University of Essex, Wivenhoe Park, Colchester CO4
Telephone: 01206 873261

Brzeska, Wallis, Nicholson Middleditch Ayrton, Spender, feature in special collection of 20th century art. Programme of six temporary exhibitions a year.

www.essex.ac.uk

HAMPSHIRE

Breamore House
Breamore nr Fordingbridge SP6
Telephone: 01725 22468

Elizabethan manor house includes 17th and 18th century art and furniture: by Teniers, van Dyck, Snyder.

www.breamorehouse.com

Broadlands
Romsey SO51
Telephone: 01794 516878

Lord Mountbatten's family residence, and in 19th century, that of Lord Palmerston, prime minister. Significant works include The Iron Forge by Joseph Wright of Derby, and collection of 18th century neo-classical statuary.

www.broadlands.net

The Vyne
Sherborne St.John
Basingstoke RG26
Telephone: 01256 883858

Built by William, First Lord Sandys in 16th century. Fine Tudor Chapel with Renaissance glass, Palladian staircase and collection of period furniture.

www.nationaltrust.org.uk/main/w-thevyne

WILTSHIRE

Fox Talbot Museum
Lacock, nr Chippenham SN15
Telephone: 01249 730459

Commemorates the discoveries of William Henry Fox Talbot, (1800-77) inventor of the photographic negative.

www.daysoutguide.co.uk/Fox-Talbot-Museum

Mompesson House
The Close Salisbury SP1
Telephone: 01722 420980

Mansion sited in the Cathedral Close. Holds Turnbull Collection of 18th century drinking glasses and china collection.

www.touruk.co.uk/houses/housewilts_momp.

Wilton House
Wilton nr Salisbury SP2
Telephone: 01722 746700

Owned by the Earls of Pembroke for 400 years, designed by Inigo Jones. Decorated with Flemish paintings of 17th century, with further works by van Dyck, Ribera, Rubens, Rembrandt, Claude and Wilson.

www.wiltonhouse.com

BATH

American Museum
Claverton Manor Bath Avon BA2
Telephone: 01225 460503

Room sets show lifestyle of Americans from 17th to 19th centuries. Displays of quilting and patchwork, pewter, glass, silverware and other fine and decorative arts.
www.americanmuseum.org

Bath Assembly Rooms
Bennett Street Bath BA1
Telephone: 01225 477173

Restored to 18th century grandeur after War-time blitz. Pump Tea rooms, Spa Waters, and the Museum of Costume housed in building.

www.bathvenues.co.uk/assembly_rooms.aspx

Bristol Museums and Art Gallery
Queens Road Bristol BS8
Telephone: 01272 223571

Works from 1300 to contemporary. Collection of paintings, glassware and Bristol Delftware. Holds The Schiller Collection of Oriental art.
www.bristol.gov.uk/museums

Clevedon Court
Tickenham Road, Clevedon BS21
Telephone: 01275 872257

Fine collection of Nailsea glass and Elton ware in 14th century manor house.

www.nationaltrust.org.uk/main/
w-findaplace/w-clevedoncourt

Holburne Museum and Crafts Study Centre
Great Pulteney Street Bath BA2
Telephone: 01225 466669

Collection of fine and applied arts gathered by Sir Thomas Holburne in 19th century. Includes bronzes, glassware and miniatures.

www.holburne.org

Royal West of England Academy
Queens Road, Clifton,
Bristol BS8
Telephone: 01272 735129

Collection of art from members of the RWA, who have included Duncan Grant, Vanessa Bell, Anne Redpath and Mary Fedden.
www.rwa.org.uk

DORSET

Bridport Museum
South Street Bridport DT6
Telephone: 01308 458703

Houses the Codd Collection and Walton Collection, and the work of Francis Newbury, all local artists of 19th century.

www.bridportmuseum.co.uk

Dorset County Museum
High West Street Dorchester
Telephone: 01305 262735

Topographical views of the local area and pictures by Dorset based artists. Some documents of renowned authors such as Thomas Hardy.

www. dorsetcountymuseum.org

Hardy's Cottage
Higher Bockhampton
nr Dorchester DT2
Telephone: 01305 262366

Author's birthplace in 1840, furnished by National Trust.

www. nationaltrust.org.uk/main/
w-findaplace/w-hardyscottage

Kingston Lacey
Wimborne Minster BH21
Telephone: 01202 883402

17th century house contains works by Titian, Rubens, Lely, van Dyck. Interesting collection of Egyptian artefacts.

www. nationaltrust.org.uk/main/
w-findaplace/w-kingstonlacy

DEVON
À La Ronde
Summer Lane, Exmouth EX8
Telephone: 01395 265514

Imaginatively designed 16 sided house, built for Jane and Mary Parminter in 18th century. Contains feather frieze and shell covered gallery.

www.qype.fr/events/110825-Jenny-Moon-A-La-Ronde-
Exmouth

Arlington Court
Arlington nr Barnstaple EX3
Telephone: 01271 850296

Georgian mansion in parkland. Early vehicles, carriages and traps, model ships and costumes from last century.

www.nationaltrust.org.uk/.../w-findaplace/w-
arlingtoncourt

Castle Drogo
Drewsteignton nr Exeter EX6
Telephone: 01647 433306

Designed by Sir Edwin Lutyens, Castle Drogo was built between 1910 and 1930. Stands over the Gorge of the River Teign.

www.infobritain.co.uk/Castle_Drogo

Killerton
Broadclyst Exeter EX5
Telephone: 01392 881345

Houses the Paul De Bush Costume Collection; period room sets including Victorian laundry.

www.devonholidayguide.co.uk/
articles/killerton

Markers Cottage
Broadclyst Exeter EX5
Telephone: 01392 461546

Medieval cob house that contains a notable screen with a period painting illustrating the life of St.Andrew.

www.nationaltrust.org.uk/main/w-vh/.../w-
killertonmarkerscottage

Overbecks
Museum and Garden
Sharpitor Salcombe TQ8
Telephone: 01548 842893

Archive of early photos of the locality, model sets of ships and boats, collection of natural objects.

www.greatbritishgardens.co.uk/overbecks

Plymouth City Museum and Art Gallery
Drake Circus Plymouth PL4
Telephone: 01752 264878

Ethnographic and natural history collections. Art of the St.Ives and Camden Town Schools. Library of two thousand antique volumes. Changing programme of temporary exhibitions.

www.plymouth.gov.uk/museum

Saltram
Plympton Plymouth PL7
Telephone: 01752 333503

George II period mansion with original contents; Chinese wallpaper, fine porcelain and furniture Paintings by Reynolds and Kauffman.

www.nationaltrust.org.uk/main/
w-saltram

ShuteBarton
Shute nr Axminster EX13
Telephone: 01752 346585

Medieval manor house with subsequent additions and alterations.

www.classicguide.co.uk/attractions/shute-barton

Torre Abbey Museum and Art Gallery
Torre Abbey, The Kings Drive,
Torquay TQ2
Telephone: 01803 293593

Period room sets house displays of silverware, pewter, glass and furniture. Paintings by Holman Hunt and Burne Jones.

www.torre-abbey.org.uk

CORNWALL

Antony
Torpoint Plymouth PL11
Telephone: 01752 812191

Portraits by Reynolds and Ramsay in special greystone mansion, home of the Carew family for six hundred years.

www.nationaltrust.org.uk/.../w-visits/
w-findaplace/w-antony

Cotehele
St.Dominick nr Saltash PL12
Telephone: 01579 351346
Home of the Edgcumbe family, house contains heirlooms of period furniture, armour, tapestries and textiles. Also maritime museum and art gallery.

www.cornwall-calling.co.uk/national-trust/cotehele

Falmouth Art Gallery
Municipal Buildings,
The Moor, Falmouth TR11
Telephone: 01326 313863

Art collection includes works by Alfred Munnings, Laura Knight, Henry Scott Tuke, and other artists associated with the locality.

www.falmouthartgallery.com

Barbara Hepworth Museum
Barnoon Hill, St.Ives TR26
Telephone: 01736 796226

House and studio of advanced abstract sculptor. Contains 50 works made from late 20s to '70s. Documents of the artist.

www.tate.org.uk/stives/hepworth

Newlyn Art Gallery
Penzance TR18
Telephone: 01736 63715

Changing programme of contemporary exhibitions.

www.newlynartgallery.co.uk

North Cornwall Museum and Gallery
The Clease, Camelford PL32
Telephone: 01840 212954

The history of Cornwall to the last century.

www.north-cornwall.com/nortcornwallmuseum

Penzance and District Museum and Art Gallery
Morrab Road, Penzance TR18
Telephone: 01736 63625

Industrial and natural history of the region. Also collection of Newlyn School of artists, from Lamorna Birch to Stanhope Forbes.

www.touruk.co.uk/cornwall/corn_pez

Royal Cornwall Museum
Royal Institution of Cornwall River Street Truro TR1
Telephone: 01872 72205

Cornish archaeology and other items of interest including decorative art from 14th century, studio pottery, costume and textiles.

www.royalcornwallmuseum.org.uk/

Tate St.Ives
Porthmeor Beach St.Ives TR26
Telephone: 01736 796226

Changing presentations of Tate Collection of St.Ives artists from 20s to present day. Temporary and touring exhibitions.

www.tate.org.uk/stives

Trerice
nr Newquay TR8
Telephone: 01637 875404
Secluded Elizabethan manor house, built 1571. Small museum.

www.cornwall-online.co.uk/heritage./trerice

Storytelling. The educational programme at Dulwich Picture Gallery

COTSWOLDS and THE MALVERNS
Oxfordshire, Gloucestershire
Herefordshire, Worcestershire, Shropshire,
Warwickshire

OXFORDSHIRE

Ashdown House
Lambourn Newbury RG16
Telephone: 01494 755569

17th century mansion holding portraits of Elizabeth, Queen of Bohemia, and the Craven family.

www.nationaltrust.org.uk/main/
w-ashdownhouse

Ashmolean Museum
Beaumont Street Oxford OX1
Telephone: 01865 553 823

Renovated from 2001 and reopened in 2009, Britain's oldest museum keeps a arge holding of ancient antiquities: Eastern, Islamic, Roman, Greek, Medieval art and artefacts. Strong in Italian Renaissance to Tieplo and Canaletto. Presents a changing programme of temporary exhibitions.

www.ashmolean.org

Blenheim Palace
Woodstock OX20
Telephone: 01993 810 500

Residence of First Duke of Marlborough, designed by Sir John Vanbrugh and Nicholas Hawksmoor. Gardens by Capability Brown. Contains family portraits, tapestries, objects, furniture.

www.blenheimpalace.com

Buscot Park
Faringdon SN7
Telephone: 0845 345 3387

18th century house with ornamental gardens. Holds the Faringdon Collection of art and antiquities.

www.buscot-park.com

Christ Church Picture Gallery
Christ Church Oxford OX1
Telephone: 01865 276172

Holds c.2000 drawings by masters from 15th to 17th century; significant paintings from Hugo van der Goes to Frans Hals; also a collection of 18th century glass.

www.chch.ox.ac.uk/gallery

Greys Court
Rotherfield Greys
Henley-On-Thames TG9
Telephone: 01494 755564

14th century fortified manor house, period contents. Well-House and Ice House. Gardens.

www.nationaltrust.org.uk/main/
w-greyscourt

Modern Art Oxford
30 Pembroke Street
Oxford OX1 2BP
Telephone: 01865 722733

Changing programme of temporary exhibitions concerned with developing contemporary art. Related educational, conference and lecture programme.

www.modernartoxford.org

Upton House
Banbury OX15
Telephone: 01295 87266

Major private collection of old masters including Breughel, Memling, Tintoretto, Guardi and Gainsborough. Tapestries and porcelain.
www.nationaltrust.org.uk/main/
w-uptonhouse

GLOUCESTERSHIRE

Chedworth Roman Villa
Yanworth nr Cheltenham GL54
Telephone: 01242 890256

Villa discovered in 1864. Contains 4th century mosaics, and other archeological finds. Also bath houses and temple.

www.nationaltrust.org.uk/chedworth/

Cheltenham Art Gallery and Museum
Clarence Street, Cheltenham GL50
Telephone: 01242 237431

Local archeology, social and natural history. Important holding of the Arts and Crafts movement: Voysey, Ashbee, Russell, and Hull Grundy Bequest. Extensive collection of art from Metsu to Stanley Spencer.

www.cheltenhamartgallery.org

Gloucester City Museum and Art Gallery
Brunswick Road, Gloucester GL1
Telephone: 01452 524131

Houses array of Celtic metalwork and Roman relics; collection of decorative objects ranging from Staffordshire pottery to Bristol glass. Extensive art collection.

www.thisisgloucestershire.co.uk/
Gloucester-City-Museum

Hailes Abbey
nr Winchcombe, Cheltenham GL54
Telephone: 01242 602398

Excavated remains of 13th century abbey with small museum of relics.

www.english-heritage.org.uk/daysout/.../hailes-abbey

Kelmscott Manor
Kelmscott n Lechlade GL7
Telephone: 01367 52486

Summer home of poet and designer William Morris from 1871-96. and DG Rossetti. Studies from Pre-Raphaelite period, furniture by Morris and Webb.

www.kelmscottmanor.org.uk

Snowshill Manor
Snowshill nr Broadway WR12
Telephone: 01386 852410

Tudor House includes Charles Paget Wade Collection of musical instruments, toys, bicycles etc.

www.nationaltrust.org.uk/main/w-snowshillmanor

HEREFORD & WORCESTER

Berrington Hall
nr Leominster HR6
Telephone: 01568 615721

Designed by Harry Holland in neo-classical manner, 18th century mansion contains Victorian laundry, dairy, and examples of period fittings and furniture.

www.britainexpress.com/counties/hereford/.../
Berrington

Churchill Gardens and Hatton Art Gallery
Venns Lane Hereford HR4
Telephone: 01432 267409

Room sets of different periods and historical costumes. The work of WWI artist Brian Hatton (1887-1916).

www.travelpod.com/The_Churchill_Gardens_Museum_
and_Hatton_Gallery

Eastnor Castle
Ledbury HR8
Telephone: 01531 633160 633160
Gothic Revival architecture, 1815; perpendicular vault designed by Pugin with Renaissance style library and furniture.

www.eastnorcastle.com

Hereford Cathedral Chained Library
The Cathedral Hereford HR1
Telephone: 01432 374200

Over 200 manuscripts from 8th to 15th century, chained books date from 17th century.

www.herefordcathedral.org

Hereford City Museum and Art Gallery
Broad Street Hereford HR4
Telephone: 01432 374202

Archaeology, natural history, the decorative and applied arts. Collection of work by local artists.

www.herefordcathedral.org

Malvern Library Art Gallery
Graham Road Great Malvern WR14
Telephone: 01684 561223

Local works of art from 19th and early 20th centuries.

www.worcestershire.whub.org.uk/.
awards/malvern-library

Worcester City Museum and Art Gallery
Foregate Street Worcester WR1
Telephone: 01905 2537

Social and natural history, archaeology, and art collection of 19th-20th centuries. Small holding of David Cox landscapes, and contemporary graphic works.

www.worcestershire.gov.ukgallery

Ironbridge Gorge Museum
Ironbridge Telford TF8
Telephone: 01952 433424

Seven museums and associated sites chart local history of iron industry. Elton Collection of industrial art. Coalport china and ceramic tiles.

www.ironbridge.org.uk

Weston Park
Weston-under-Lizard TF11
Telephone: 01952 850430

Portraits by Holbein, van Dyck, Hoppner, Stubbs and Gainsborough; porcelain and period furniture, in 17th century house.

www.weston-park.com

SOMERSET

Brympton d'Evercy
Brympton nr Yeovil BA22
Telephone: 01935 862528

Family portraits from Kneller to Lawrence in Tudor mansion.

www.brymptonhouse.co.uk

King John's Hunting Lodge
The Square Axbridge BS2
Telephone: 01934 732012

Tudor merchant's house, now run as a small local museum.

www.nationaltrust.org.uk/main/
w-kingjohnshuntinglodge

Montacute House
Montacute TA15
Telephone: 01935 823289

H-Plan Elizabethan mansion with well preserved original features; stained glass and ornamental plasterwork. 17th century Samplers, Tudor and Jacobean portraits.

www.nationaltrust.org.uk/...montacute/
w-montacute-house

The Museum of South Somerset
Hendford Yeovil BA20
Telephone: 01935 24774

Roman room sets, archaeology, social history. Collection of period costume, paintings from 18th to 20th centuries.

www.southsomersetmuseums.org.uk

STAFFORDSHIRE

Moseley Old Hall
Moseley Old Hall Lane, Fordhouses,
Wolverhampton WV10
Telephone: 01902 782808

Elizabethan mansion with special historical display of Charles II and the Battle of Worcester.

www.nationaltrust.org.uk/main/
w-moseleyoldhall

Shugborough
Milford nr Stafford ST17
Telephone: 01889 881388

Seat of the Earls of Lichfield. Numerous collection of silverware, paintings and furniture. Utility rooms in traditional working order. Gardens and Park.

www.nationaltrust.org.uk/main/
w-shugboroughestate

Shire Hall Gallery
Market Square Stafford ST16
Telephone: 01785 278345

Work by local artists, small crafts and jewellery collection. Changing programme of twenty exhibitions a year.

www.staffordshire.gov.uk/leisure/
museumandgalleries/shirehallgalleries/

WARWICKSHIRE

Arbury Hall
Arbury Nuneaton CV10
Telephone: 024 7638 2804

Gothic revival mansion of late 18th century, holds works by Lely, Reynolds, Romney, and furniture by Chippendale.

www.arburyestate.co.uk

Charlecote Park
Warwick CV35
Telephone: 01789 470277

Lucy Family residence since 1247. Present mansion built in 1550s with interesting interiors of 1820s in the Romantic style. Items from William Beckford's Fonthill Abbey.

www.nationaltrust.org.uk/
w-charlecotepark

Coughton Court
nr Alcester B49
Telephone: 01789 762435
Elizabethan house, centre of conflict in English civil war, and connections with The Gunpowder Plot. Family portraits and heirlooms of the Throckmorton family; childrens period costume display.

www.coughtoncourt.co.uk

Mead Gallery
Arts Centre University of Warwick
Coventry CV4
Telephone: 024765 74179

Rugby Collection of Post-war British Art. Programme of temporary exhibitions.

www.warwick.ac.uk/services/art/meadgallery

Packwood House
Lapworth Solihull B94
Telephone: 01564 783294

Collection of 16th century textiles and furniture held in converted mansion of the period.

www.touruk.co.uk/houses/housewarw_pack

Upton House
Banbury OX15
Telephone: 01295 670266

17th century mansion contains Lord Bearsteds personal collection of tapestries, Sevres porcelain, furnitureand works of art.

www.touruk.co.uk/houses/housewarw_upton

Warwick Castle
Warwick CV34
Telephone: 01926 495421

State rooms contain arms and armour, furniture, paintings by Rubens and van Dyck. Parkland designed by Capability Brown.

www.warwick-castle.co.uk

NORTHAMPTONSHIRE

Canons Ashby House
Canons Ashby nr Daventry NN11
Telephone: 0137 860044

Dryden family home from 16th century. Features include wall paintings and Jacobean plasterwork.

www.aboutbritain.com/CanonsAshbyHouse

Cottesbrooke Hall
Cottesbrooke NN6
Telephone: 01604 505808

Reputed setting for Jane Austen's Mansfield Park. Contains array of European period furniture, porcelain, and 18th/19th century sporting art.

www.cottesbrookehall.co.uk

Lyveden New Bield
nr Oundle Peterborough PE8
Telephone: 01832 205358

Lodge begun by Sir Thomas Tresham in 1595. Contains 17th century biblical friezes.

www.theaa.com/days-out/northamptonshire-lyveden-new-bield

Central Museum and Art Gallery
Guildhall Road Northampton NN1
Telephone: 01604 838 111

Works from 16th to 20th century; collections of applied arts, social and natural history. Changing programme of temporary exhibitions.

www.northampton.gov.uk/museums

LEICESTERSHIRE

Belvoir Castle
Belvoir nr Grantham NG32
Telephone: 01476 871002

Major works by Poussin, Murillo, Gainsborough, and Gobelins Tapestries.
www.belvoircastle.com

Leicestershire Museum and Art Gallery
New Walk Leicester LE1
Telephone: 01533 554100

17th to 20th century paintings from Carraci to Lowry, special aspects of German Expressionist art, and ceramics by Rie and Cowper.
www.leicester.gov.uk/museums

Staunton Harold Church
Staunton Harold, Asby de la Zouch
Telephone: 01332 863822

17th century church retains original details and furnishings.

www.derbyshireuk.net/staunton

LINCOLNSHIRE

Belton House
Grantham NG32
Telephone: 01476 66116

Built 1685-88 for Sir John Brownlow, house contains portraits, tapestries, porcelain and silverware.

www.touruk.co.uk/houses/houselincs_belt

Burghley House
Stamford PE9
Telephone: 01780 52451

Built 1546-87 for William Cecil, First Lord Burghley. Extensive decorative art by 17th century Antonio Verrio. Large collection of oriental ceramics; carvings by Grinling Gibbons.

www.burghley.co.uk

Fulbeck Hall
Grantham NG32
Telephone: 01400 72205

Georgian house contains variety of 17th to 19th century paintings, from Zuccarelli to Rowe. Education programme.

www.touruk.co.uk/houses/houselincs_fulb

Grimsthorpe Castle
Grimsthorpe Bourne PE10
Telephone: 01778 591205

Part designed by Sir John Vanbrugh in 1726. Major holding of historical portraits and furnishings. Chapel decorated by Jacob de Wet.

www.grimsthorpe.co.uk

Gunby Hall
Gunby nr Spilsby PE23
Telephone: 07870 758876

Period furniture, portraits by Reynolds. Walled garden.

www.gunbyhall.ic24.net

Woolsthorpe Manor
23 Newton Way, Woolsthorpe-by-Colsterworth NG23
Telephone: 01476 860338

Birthplace of Sir Isaac Newton, and of his major works (Principia Mathematica, pub.1687).

www.nationaltrust.org.uk/
w-woolsthorpemanor

SUFFOLK

Christchurch Mansion
Christchurch Park, Ipswich IP4
Telephone: 01473 433554

Suffolk artists from Gainsborough to Constable, also decorative art collection; ceramics, glassware, clocks and furniture.

www.ipswich.gov.uk/Services/Christchurch+Mansion

Ickworth House
Ickworth, The Rotunda, Horringer,
Bury St Edmunds IP29
Telephone: 01284 735270

Paintings by Titian, Velázquez, Gainsborough. Extensive Georgian silver collection.

www. nationaltrust.org.uk/main/
w-ickworthhouse

Guildhall of Corpus Christi
Market Place Lavenham Sudbury CO10
Telephone: 01787 247646

Tudor building houses room sets charting 700 years of local history, and development of the wool trade.

_www.nationaltrust.org.uk/main/
w-lavenham

NORFOLK

Blickling Hall
Blickling Norwich NR1
Telephone: 01263 738030

Early 17th century mansion houses tapestries, furniture and pictures. Ornamental plasterwork in Long Gallery.

www.aboutbritain.com/BlicklingHall

Elizabethan House Museum
4 South Quay Great Yarmouth NR30
Telephone: 01493 855746

A museum of domestic life in 16th century building.

www.nationaltrust.org.uk/main/
w-elizabethanhousemuseum

Felbrigg Hall
Felbrigg Norwich NR11
Telephone: 01263 837444

Imposing 17th century house with original furnishings and paintings.

www.norfolkcoast.co.uk/articles/felbriggHall

Gainsborough's House
46 Gainsborough Street
Sudbury CO10
Telephone: 01787 372958

Major collection of Gainsborough paintings, drawings, prints. Changing programme of exhibitions.

www.gainsborough.org

Holkham Hall
Wells-next-the-Sea NR23
Telephone: 01328 710227

Neo-classical mansion by William Kent. Thomas Coke Collection includes Carracci, Rubens, Claude, Poussin, Gainsborough.

www.holkham.co.uk

St Georges Guildhall
27 King Street
Kings Lynn PE30
Telephone: 01553 765565

Large English Medieval Guildhall, now used as an arts centre.

www.daysoutguide.co.uk/
st-georges-guildhall

Sainsbury Centre for Visual Arts
University of East Anglia
Norwich NR4
Telephone: 01603 591033

Centre of World Art Studies & Museology. Collections include: art nouveau, commercial art, and the Robert and Liza Sainsbury Collection including Moore, Giacometti, Bacon.

www.scva.org.uk

Sandringham House
Sandringham, Kings Lynn PE35
Telephone: 01553 612908

Private residence of HM The Queen. Holds tapestries, Royal Edwardian and Victorian portraits.

www. royal.gov.uk/SandringhamHouse/
SandringhamHouse

NOTTINGHAMSHIRE

Clumber Park
The Estate Office Clumber Park
Worksop S80
Telephone: 01909 544917

Gothic Revival chapel 1886-89, pleasure gardens, exhibition of utilitarian objects.

www.nationaltrust.org.uk/w-clumberpark

Nottingham Castle Museum and Art Gallery
The Castle Nottingham NG1
Telephone: 0844 4775678

Regimental collection, social history and archeology. 18th to 19th century schools of local artists.

www.nottinghamcity.gov.uk/museums

Mr Straw's House
1 Blyth Grove Worksop S81
Telephone: 01909 482380

Turn of century house with preserved interior of period furnishings and decoration.

www.aboutbritain.com/Mr StrawsHouse

THE MIDLANDS
Cheshire & Merseyside

CHESHIRE

Arley Hall
Arley nr Northwich CW9
Telephone: 01565 777353
Early Victorian house; accent in extensive private collection on topographical watercolours of local country houses.
www.arleyhallandgardens.com

Capesthorne Hall
Macclesfield SK11
Telephone: 01625 861221

Paintings by Allan Ramsay, and other masters. Period furniture and memorabilia.

www.capesthorne.com

Dunham Massey
Altrincham WA1
Telephone: 0161 9411025

Georgian House and residence of Last Earl of Stamford to 1976. Thirty rooms contain period furniture, Hugenot silver, paintings, library.

www.nationaltrust.org.uk/main/w-findaplace/w-dunhammassey

Grovesnor Museum
27 Grovesnor Street Chester CH1
Telephone: 01244 321616
Topographical views, sporting scenes, collections of silver, local paintings and archaeological items.

www. chester.gov.uk/culture_and_leisure/grosvenor_museum

Little Moreton Hall
Congleton CW12
Telephone: 01260 272018

Built 1450-1580, Tudor manor house includes Elizabethan Long Gallery with period wall paintings in the Great Hall.

www.theheritagetrail.co.uk/manor houses/little moreton

Lyme Park
Disley Stockport SK12
Telephone: 01663 762023

Residence of Legh family for 600 years. Period interiors reflect changing styles over the centuries. Mortlake Tapestries, Grinling Gibbons carvings.

www.touruk.co.uk/houses/house-cheshire-lyme-park

Quarry Bank Mill
Wilmslow SK9
Telephone: 01625 445896

Georgian Cotton Mill built 1784, now functions as crafts workshops and textile museum. Repeats the conditions of original industrial activity.

www.quarrybankmill.org.uk

Tabley House
Knutsford WA16
Telephone: 01565 750151
Paintings by Turner, Devis, Fuseli, Thompson and Ward in extensive private collection.

www.tableyhouse.co.uk

Tatton Park
Knutsford WA16
Telephone: 01625 374400

Regency house with significant holding of old masters from Canaletto to van Dyck, Veronese and Raphael. Also collections of glass, china and decorative objects.

www.tattonpark.org.uk

Warrington Museum and Art Gallery
Bold Street Warrington WA1
Telephone: 01925 442733

Ethnographic, geological collections. Work by local artists, some Dutch and Norwich School painters.

www. museum.warrington.gov.uk

West Park Museum
Prestbury Road Macclesfield
Telephone: 01625 610831

Egyptian antiquities, local history, Victorian paintings.
www.aboutbritain.com/WestParkMuseum.htm

WEST MIDLANDS

Bantock House Museum
Bantock Park, Bradmore Road,
Wolverhampton WV3
Telephone: 01902 552195

Houses The Balston Collection of Staffordshire figures, also 18th century enamels, and decorative objects from early 19th century.

www.wolverhamptonart.org.uk/bantock

The Barber Institute of Fine Arts
University of Birmingham Edgbaston
Birmingham B15
Telephone: 0121 414 7333

Founded 1932, institute houses University collections of art from 14th century drawings to early 20th century. Occasional exhibitions of selected works from the collection.

www.barber.org.uk

Birmingham Museum and Art Gallery
Chamberlain Square
Birmingham B3
Telephone: 0121 2352834

Western paintings from medieval to early 20th century artists: Delacroix, Fantin-Latour, Pissarro, Bomberg, Sutherland. Exhibition and education programme.

www. bmag.org.uk

New Art Gallery Walsall
Gallery Square
Walsall, West Midlands WS2 8LG
Telephone: 01922 654 400

Houses the Garman-Ryan Collection, including works by Epstein, Freud, Degas, van Gogh, Blake, Durer.

www.thenewartgallerywalsall.org.uk

Wolverhampton Art Gallery and Museum
Lichfield Street Wolverhampton WV1
Telephone: 01902 552055

Ranges from 18th century British to Anglo-American Pop Art of the 1960s. Works by Wadsworth, Grant, Nash, Spencer.

www.wolverhamptonart.org.uk

Initial Access
Units 19 and 20
Calibre Industrial Park Laches Close
Off Enterprise Drive Four Ashes
Wolverhampton WV10 7DZ
Telephone: 01902 790419

Collection of experimental work formed by Frank Cohen. A changing programme of exhibitions presents cutting edge sculpture and installations by international artists.
www.initialaccess.co.uk

MERSEYSIDE

Lady Lever Art Gallery
Port Sunlight Village, Wirral L62
Telephone: 0151 478 4136

Founded by the First Viscount Leverhulme in 1922, the Gallery contains an extensive collection of 18th century furniture, Chinese ceramics, and works by 18th and 19th century masters, from Reynolds to Burne Jones.

www.liverpoolmuseums.org.uk/ladylever

Sudley Art Gallery
Mossley Hill Road Liverpool L18
Telephone: 0151 7243245

Includes The Holt bequest of works by Landseer, Millais and Holman Hunt. Also some 18th century paintings.

www.liverpoolmuseums.org.uk/sudley

Tate Liverpool
Albert Dock Liverpool L3
Telephone: 0151 702 7400

Venue for touring exhibitions from Tate, London, and special projects by artists-in-residence. Education and lecture programme.

www.tate.org.uk/liverpool

University of Liverpool Art Gallery
3 Abercromby Square
Liverpool L69
Telephone: 0151 794 2348

Established 1977, gallery keeps major collections of art in all media, from Turner and Girtin to contemporary British artists; Hockney, Denny.

www.liv.ac.uk/artgall/gallery

Walker Art Gallery
William Brown Street L3
Telephone: 0151 478 4199

Significant holding of Western art from 14th century to 20th century. Italian masters: Martini, de Roberti, Signorelli; Rembrandt, Poussin, Rubens. English 18th century artists strongly represented.

www.liverpoolmuseums.org.uk/walker

Speke Hall
The Walk, Liverpool L24
Telephone: 0844 800 4799

Tudor mansion decorated with period furnishings, and some ornamental details.

www. nationaltrust.org.uk/w-visits/
w-findaplace/w-spekehall

DERBYSHIRE

Bakewell Old House Museum
Cunningham Place
Bakewell DE45
Telephone: 01629 813165

Period features in 16th century house. Costume collection with lace and samplers, children's toys.

www.culture24.org.uk/em000014

Bolsover Castle
Castle Street Bolsover S44
Telephone: 01246 345777

Interesting aspects include the Little Castle, which is decorated with carvings, frescoes and murals.

www.derbyshireuk.net/bolsover_castle

Calke Abbey
Ticknall Derby DE73
Telephone: 01332 863822

Period room sets, natural history collections, fine furniture.

www.theheritagetrail.co.uk/stately homes/calke abbey

Chatsworth
Bakewell DE45
Telephone: 01246 565300

Contains five state rooms with unaltered 17th century interiors and furnishings. Twenty four further rooms open to visitors. Tapestries, library of 17000 volumes, paintings by Rembrandt, Hals, van Dyck, Tintoretto up to Lucian Freud. Also silver and porcelain.

www. chatsworth.org

Derby Museum and Art Gallery
The Strand, Derby DE1
Telephone: 01332 641901

Major holding of Joseph Wrightof Derby (1734-97), painter of the Industrial Revolution. Also collection of Derby Porcelain, natural, social and military history.

www. derby.gov.uk/museums

Eyam Hall
Eyam Sheffield S30
Telephone: 01433 631976

Ancestral home of the Wright family, built 1671. Contains Jacobean tapestries, family portraits, and period utensils.

www. eyamhall.co.uk

Hardwick Hall
Doe Lea Chesterfield
Telephone: 01246 850430
Built in late 16th century for Bess of Hardwick, contains tapestries and needlework from 1601.

www. hardwickhallhotel.co.uk

Kedleston Hall
Quarndon Derby DE22
Telephone: 01332 842191
Neo-classical mansion built for the Curzon family 1759-65. Robert Adam designed state rooms reflect the age of elegance.

www.heritage.elettra.co.uk/kedleston

Pickfords House Museum
41 Friargate Derby DE1
Telephone: 01332 255363

Historic costume, Derby porcelain, pictures by Wright of Derby and Benjamin West.

www.derby.gov.uk/museums

Renishaw Hall
Sheffield S31
Telephone: 01246 432310

Sitwell family home; Italianate gardens, follies and small museum.

www.renishaw-hall.co.uk

Sudbury Hall
Ashbourne DE6
Telephone: 01283 585305

Ornamental carvings by Gibbons and Pierce, decorative paintings by Laguerre. Imposing staircase.

www.derbyshireuk.net/sudbury_hall

YORKSHIRE

The Bar Convent Museum
17 Blossom Street York YO2
Telephone: 01904 643238
Religious history of the area, artefacts of the order from 15th century onwards.

www.bar-convent.org

Beningborough Hall
Shipton-by-Beningborough
York Y06
Telephone: 01904 472027

Built 1716, contains paintings loaned by National Portrait Gallery, London. Richly decorated interior.

www. nationaltrust.org.uk/
beningbroughhallandgardens

Cartwright Hall
Lister Park Bradford BD9
Telephone: 01274 432626

19th and 20th century British art, from Pre-Raphaelites to Sir William Rothenstein and the British Impressionists. Changing programme of exhibitions.

www.bradfordmuseums.org

Castle Howard
Telephone: 01653 648640

Period costume from 18th century to the present day. Changing displays.

www.castlehoward.co.uk

**Doncaster Museum and
Art Gallery**
Chequer Road Doncaster DN1
Telephone: 01302 736000

16th to 19th century paintings; Flemish and Dutch Schools, and collection of English decorative arts.

www.doncaster.gov.uk/museums

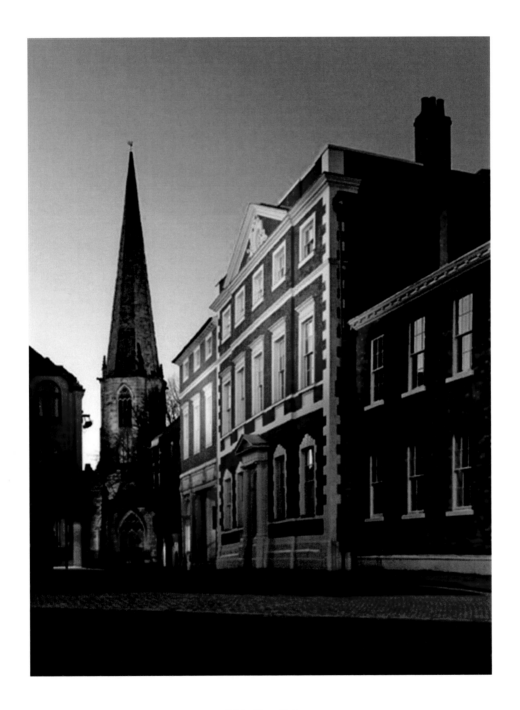

Fairfax House York
York Conservation Archive

East Riddlesden Hall
Bradford Road Keighley BD20
Telephone: 01535 607075

17th century manor house with collection of pewter and embroideries, with local period furniture.

www.eastriddlesdenhall.co.uk

Fairfax House
Castlegate York YO1
Telephone: 01904 655543

Noel Terry Collection of period furniture and clocks in 18th century mansion.

www.fairfaxhouse.co.uk

Graves Art Gallery
48 Arundel Gate
Sheffield S1 2PP
Telephone: 0114 278 2600

Strong holding of French painters: Corot, Cezanne, Monet, Matisse. Works by The Camden Town Group, and collections of Far Eastern, Asian and African Art.

www.museums-sheffield.org.uk

Harewood House
Harewood Leeds LS17
Telephone: 0113 218 1010

Lascelles family residence since 18th century. Ornate decorative interior by Kauffmann and Zucchi. Chippendale furniture, paintings by Gainsborough, Hoppner, Lawrence.

www.harewood.org

Leeds City Art Gallery
The Headrow, Leeds LS1
Telephone: 0113 247 8256

Works by Frank Dobson and Henry Moore, crafts collection and changing programme of temporary exhibitions.

www.leeds.gov.uk/artgallery

Lotherton Hall
Aberford Leeds LS25
Telephone: 01532 813259

Edwardian mansion owned by Gascoigne family, contains fine and applied arts collection: Pugin, Batoni, Burges.

www.leeds.gov.uk/lothertonhall

National Media Museum
Bradford BD1 1NQ
Telephone: 0844 856 3797

Collection of media history: displays and archives of key programmes and movies from 1890s to present day.

www.nationalmediamuseum.org.uk

Nunnington Hall
Nunnington York YO6
Telephone: 01439 748283

17th century manor house reflects Yorkshire different periods in collection of miniature room sets.

www. nationaltrust.org.uk/main/w-nunningtonhall

Nostell Priory
Doncaster Road Nostell
nr Wakefield WF4
Telephone: 01924 865892

Neo-Palladian mansion completed by Robert Adam in 1760s. Paintings by Poussin, Hogarth, Kauffmann.

www.nationaltrust.org.uk/main/
w-nostellpriory

Sutton Park
Sutton-on-the-Forest,
York YO6
Telephone: 01347 810249

Collection of period furniture decorative objects and paintings.

www.statelyhome.co.uk

Rielvaux Terrace & Temples
Rielvaux, Helmsley York YO6
Telephone: 01439 798340

Elaborately decorated 18th century temples with period furniture.

www.nationaltrust.org.uk/main/
w-rievaulxterrace_temples

Smith Art Gallery
Halifax Road Brighouse
Telephone: 01422 288065

Victorian painters including Atkinson Grimshaw, and some examples of Dutch 17th century paintings.

www. calderdale.gov.uk/leisure/galleries/smith-art

Temple Newsam House
Leeds LS15
Telephone: 0113 264 5535

16th century mansion in park designed by Capability Brown. Collection includes silver, ceramics, wallpaper designs, textiles from 16th to 189th centuries. Some period portraits and modern sculptures.

www.leeds.gov.uk/templenewsam

The Stanley & Audrey Burton Gallery
University of Leeds
Parkinson Building, Woodhouse Lane, Leeds, LS2
Telephone: 0113 343 2778

19th and 20th century art, from Camden Town Group to Artist-Fellows of the University.

www.leeds.ac.uk/gallery/gallery

Treasurer's House
Chapter House Street York YO1
Telephone: 01904 624247

Town house holds the Frank Green Collection of art and artefacts from different periods.

www.nationaltrust.org.uk/main/
w-treasurershouseyork

The Hepworth Gallery
Wentworth Terrace Wakefield WF1
Telephone: 01924 305900

Modern British art from Barbara Hepworth to Henry Moore; also paintings by early 20th century artists, Sickert, Ginner, Gore and others.

www.hepworthwakefield.com/

York City Art Gallery
Exhibition Square York YO1
Telephone: 01904 687687

Art from 14th to 20th century includes paintings by Domenichino, van Goyen, MelŽndez, Whistler. Presents a changing programme of temporary exhibitions.

www.yorkartgallery.org.uk

Yorkshire Museum
Museum Gardens York YO1
Telephone: 01904 687687

Collection ranges from medieval sculpture to ceramics, jewellery, natural history and geology.

www.yorkshiremuseum.org.uk

Yorkshire Sculpture Park
Bretton Hall West Bretton Wakefield WF4
Telephone: 01924 832631

Major site for presentations of post-war British sculpture. Changing programme of exhibitions ranges from Moore, Caro, Paolozzi, Frink, to emerging artists.

www.ysp.co.uk

GREATER MANCHESTER

Bolton Museum and Art Gallery
Le Mans Crescent, Bolton BL1
Telephone:

17th century to 20th century masters including: Romanelli and Giordano, Hepworth, Auerbach, Moore and Paolozzi. Displays of English and other antiquities, and ethnographic collections.

www.boltonmuseums.org.uk

Bury Art Gallery and
Museum
Moss Street, Bury,
Greater Manchester
Telephone: 0161 253 5878

19th and 20th century paintings by Turner, Constable, Landseer, Holman Hunt, from the Thomas Wrigley collection.

www. bury.gov.uk /Leisure /

Heaton Hall
Heaton Park, Prestwich M25
Telephone: 0161 773 1085

The residence of Sir Thomas Egerton, First Earl of Wilton in the late 18th century, now owned by the City of Manchester. Contains period interiors, art and furniture.

www.heatonpark.org.uk/heatonpark

Manchester Art Gallery
Mosley Street Manchester M2
Telephone: 0161 235 8888

Collection includes works of fine and dec orative art by William Burges, Thomas Toft, John Souch, John Waterhouse and Ford Madox Brown; spanning 17th to 20th Centuries.

www.manchestergalleries.org

Gallery Oldham
Union Street Oldham Greater
Manchester OL1
Telephone: 0161 770 4653

Paintings by Rossetti, Millais, Bonington, Cox, Turner, and modern collection from Epstein to Auerbach. Changing programme of exhibitions.

www.galleryoldham.org.uk

Rochdale Art Gallery
Esplanade Rochdale Greater
Manchester OL16
Telephone: 01706 92 4492

Exhibitions by international artists; houses collection of 19yth to 20th century works by Bell, Grant Ayres. Education programme

www.culture24.org.uk/nw000118

Salford Museum and Art Gallery
Peel Park The Crescent Salford Greater Manchester M5
Telephone: 0161 778 0800

Particular holding of local artists LS Lowry (1887-1976), who charted the changing face of the industrial landscape.

www.salford.gov.uk/salfordmuseum

The Whitworth Art Gallery
University of Manchester,
Oxford Road M15
Telephone: 0161 275 7450

Collection of applied and decorative arts: textiles, wallpapers, weaving and embroidery from 4th century to date. A wide-ranging art collection of prints, paintings and sculpture, with a changing programme of temporary exhibitions.

www.whitworth.manchester.ac.uk

Wythenshawe Hall
Wythenshawe Park, Northenden,
Manchester M23
Telephone: 0161-998 2331

Four hundred year old mansion, and ancestral home of the Tatton family, houses arms and armour, ceramics, furniture, prints and paintings.

www.manchestergalleries.org

LANCASHIRE

Astley Hall
Astley Park Chorley PR7
Telephone: 01257 515151.

16th century house contains period furniture with fine and decorative art.

www.chorley.gov.uk/astleyhall

Brownsholme Hall
Clitheroe BB7
Telephone: 01254 827166

Family portraits by Devis, Reynolds, Romney, and collections of furniture, armour, stained glass, textiles.

www.browsholme.co.uk

Gawthorpe Hall
Padiham nr Burnley BB12
Telephone: 01282 771004

Houses the Rachel Kay-Shuttleworth Collection of Textiles, with loan portraits from National Portrait Gallery.

www.nationaltrust.org.uk/main/
w-gawthorpehall

Harris Museum and Art Gallery
Market Square Preston PR1
Telephone: 01772 58248

18th century glassware and ceramics are included in the displays of social history. Paintings and sculptures from mid-victorian to contemporary works.

www.culture24.org.uk/nw000085

Lancaster City Museum
Market Square Lancaster LA1
Telephone: 01772 534061

Archaeology, social and maritime history. Local artists in collection.

www. lancashire.gov.uk/acs/museums/lancastercity

Peter Scott Gallery
Lancaster University, Lancaster LA1
Telephone: 01524 594151

University owns works by Joan Miro, Kupka, Frost, Winifred Nicholson, and continues to acquire new work by leading artists.

www. lancs.ac.uk/depts/peterscott/scott

Rossendale Museum
Whitaker Park Rawstenstall
Rossendale BB4
Telephone: 01772 534061

Local history recorded in changing styles of costume, furniture and decorative arts.

www. lancashire.gov.uk/acs/sites/museums/
venues/rossendale

Rufford Old Hall
Rufford nr Ormskirk L40
Telephone: 01704 821254

16th and 17th century oak furniture, arms and armour and tapestries.

www. nationaltrust.org.uk/main/
w-ruffordoldhall

HUMBERSIDE
*Northumberland, Tyne and Wear,
Durham, Cleveland*

Ferens Art Gallery
Queen Victorial Square,
Hull HU1
Telephone: 01482 300 300

Marine and topographical paintings; Dutch and Flemish masters, Victorian and 20th Century British artists figure strongly in the collection. Programme of temporary exhibitions.

www.hullcc.gov.uk/museums/ferens

University of Hull Art Collection
The Middleton Hall, University
of Hull, Cottingham Road,
Hull HU6
Telephone: 01482-465192

Camden Town and Bloomsbury Groups, Sickeryt, Steer, Pisarro, and the Thompson Collection of ceramics.

www. 2.hull.ac.uk/fass/arts

Gray Art Gallery and Museum
Clarence Road Hartlepool TS24
Telephone: 01429 266522

Decorative arts collection includes Far Eastern antiquities,and 19th century British paintings.

www. thisishartlepool.co.uk/attractions/artgallery

Middlesborough Art Gallery
320 Linthorpe Road
Middlesborough TS1
Telephone: 01642 247445

20th century British art: Burra, Auerbach, Spencer, Frink. Changing programme of twenty exhibitions a year.

www. agreatplacetosee.com/2630/
Middlesborough_Art_Gallery

Ormesby Hall
Ormesby Middlesborough TS7
Telephone: 01642 324188

18th century house owned by Pennyman family. Ornamental interior details in wood and plaster.

www. nationaltrust.org.uk/w-visits/w-findaplace/w-ormesbyhall

---

TYNE & WEAR

Bessie Surtees House
41-44 Sandhill Newcastle
Telephone: 0191 261 1585

Two merchant's houses from 16th and 17th century near the Tyne & Wear Bridge, form classic examples of Jacobean period design.

www. english-heritage.org.uk/properties/bessie-surtees-house

NEWCASTLE

Gibside
Nr Rowlands Gill, Burnopfield NE16
Telephone: 01207 541820

Palladian Chapel with broad landscaped walks along the River Derwent.

www.nationaltrust.org.uk/w-visits/
w-findaplace/w-gibside

Hatton Gallery
The Quadrangle, University of Newcastle upon Tyne
NE1
Telephone: 0191 222 6057

Notable collection from the Renaissance to the present day. Houses late work by Kurt Schwitters, of a surrealist wall originally sited in the Lake District.

www. bbc.co.uk/arts/powerofart/cities/newcastle

Hylton Castle
Sunderland, Tyne & Wear
Telephone: 0191 261 1585

15th century gate-house with display of medieval heraldry.

www.bbc.co.uk/wear/content/hylton_castle

Laing Art Gallery
Higham Place,
Newcastle upon Tyne NE1
Telephone: 0191 232 6789

Changing programme of contemporary exhibitions and art conferences.

www.twmuseums.org.uk/laing

University Gallery
University of Northumbria, Library
Building, Sabdyford Road,
Newcastle upon Tyne NE1

Telephone: 0191 227 4424

Collection of Modern British art: Sean Scully, Norman Adams, Graham Crowley. Changing exhibitions through year.

www.northumbria.ac.uk/universitygallery

Scunthorpe Museum and Art Gallery
Oswald Road Scunthorpe DN15
Telephone: 01724 843533

Natural and social history, archaeology, displays of development of local steel industry.

ww.gofind.co.uk/scunthorpe/museums

NORTHUMBERLAND

Alnwick Castle
Alnwick Northumberland NE66
Telephone: 01665 510777

Owned by the Percy Family, Dukes of Northumberland since 1309. Furnished in Renaissance fashion, with strong holding of paintings from van Dyck to Turner. Special collection of Meissen porcelain.

www.alnwickcastle.com

Bamburgh Castle
Bamburgh NE65
Telephone: 01668 214515

Houses the John George Joicey Museum with its collections of armour, fine furniture, applied and decorative arts.

www.bamburghcastle.com

Belsay Castle
Belsay nr Ponteland NE20
Telephone: 01661 881033

Mansion designed and built for Sir Charles Monck in 19th century in neo-classical style. Guided tours.

www.northofthetyne.co.uk/Belsay

Berwick Barracks
The Parade, Berwick-on-Tweed TD15
Telephone: 0870 333 1181
Museum of the Kings Own Borderers and other presentations of local history.

www.berwick.org.uk/berwick/barracks

Bowes Museum
Barnard Castle
Co Durham DL12
Telephone: 01833 690606

Barnard Castle contains collections of fine and decorative arts accumulated by John and Josephine Bowes. Extensive displays of European costume, silver, toys, musical instruments.

www.thebowesmuseum.org.uk

Cherryburn
Station Bank, Mickley, Stocksfield NE43
Telephone: 01661 843276

Birthplace of renowned 18th century engraver and naturalist Thomas Bewick. Museum charts his life and work with technical demonstrations of printmaking methods.

www.nationaltrust.org.uk/main/
w-cherryburn

Chester Roman Fort & Museum
Chollerford, Humshaugh, Hexham on Wye NE46
Telephone: 01434 681379

Remains of Roman Fort and Bath House; contains relics of Roman sculpture and inscriptions.

www.aboutscotland.co.uk/hadrian/chesters

Cragside House
Rothbury, Morpeth
Telephone: 01669 620333

Norman Shaw house built for the First Lord Armstrong 1864-95. Holds range of Pre-Raphaelite works and original furniture.

www.nationaltrust.org.uk/w-
cragsidehousegardenandestate

Housesteads Fort & Museum
Housesteads, Haydon Bridge,
Hexham NE47
Telephone: 01434 344525

Remains of Roman Wall and outbuildings; display of found items, votive altars and original inscriptions.

www. english-heritage.org.uk/housesteads-
roman-fort-hadrians-wall/

The Lady Waterford Hall
Ford, Berwick on Tweed TD15
Telephone: 01890 820503

Murals in former School Hall by Louisa, Marchioness of Waterford, featuring local residents and their children in biblical episodes.

www. discovertheborders.co.uk/places/59

Seaton Delaval Hall
Seaton Sluice, Whitley Bay NE26
Telephone: 0191 237 9100

Major neo-baroque mansion by Sir John Vanbrugh, begun in 1718 for Admiral George Delaval. Palladian villa and imposing stables.

www.seatondelaval.org.uk/Hall.html

Wallington
Cambo, Morpeth NE61
Telephone: 01670 773967

Porcelain, furniture, pictures and period room sets with nursery and original dolls houses.

www.culture24.org.uk/ne000073

CUMBRIA

Abbott Hall Art Gallery
Kirkland Kendal LA9
Telephone: 01539 722464

Centre for contemporary and historical art housed in Georgian mansion. Collection of period portraits and furniture and changing temporary exhibitions.

www.abbothall.org.uk

Beatrix Potter Gallery
Main Street Hawkshead LA22
Telephone: 01539 436355

Beatrix Potter's original illustrations for childrens story books presented in changing selections of drawings and watercolours.

www.nationaltrust.org.uk/main/
w-beatrixpottergallery

Beatrix Potter's Lake District
Packhorse Court Keswick CA12
Telephone: 0844 504 1233

Environment of miniature tableaux and videos which tell the story of Beatrix Potter's life and creations.

www.hop-skip-jump.com

Brantwood
Coniston LA21
Telephone: 015394 41396

Home of critic and philosopher John Ruskin from 1872 to 1900, and centre for intellectual developments of the time. Contains collection of Ruskins watercolours and drawings.

www.brantwood.org.uk

Carlisle Cathedral
Carlisle CA3
Telephone: 01228 548151

Founded in 1122 the Cathedral contains medieval stained glass, carvings and painted panels. Also holds silverware and other ecclesiastical treasures.

www.carlislecathedral.org.uk

Dalemain
Penrith CA11
Telephone: 01768 486450

Georgian mansion with relics of earlier periods of design. Features include 18th century Chinese wallpaper, family holdings and regimental collection of Westmoreland and Cumberland Yeomanry.

www.dalemain.com

Furness Abbey
Barrow in Furness LH13
Telephone: 01229 823420

Museum and exhibition in Cistercian Abbey founded in 1123 by Stephen, King of England.

www.visitcumbria.com/sl/furnabb

Holker Hall
Cark-in-Cartmel
Grange-over-Sands LA11
Telephone: 015395 58328

Cavendish family residence developed in 19th century by 7th Duke of Devonshire. Furniture from Louis XV to Victorian pieces. Paintings and memorabilia.

www.holker-hall.co.uk

Hutton in the Forest
Penrith CA11
Telephone: 01768 484449

Home of Inglewood family from 1605. Collections of paintings, furniture, ceramics and tapestries.

www.hutton-in-the-forest.co.uk

Levens Hall
Kendal LA8
Telephone: 01539 560321

Elizabethan manor contains Jacobean furniture, decorative interiors, Cordova leather wall coverings and early English patchwork.

www.levenshall.co.uk/levens_hall

Muncaster Castle
Ravenglass CA18
Telephone: 01229 717614

Penington Family estate since 1208. Includes Octagonal Library by Salvin, fine needlework and tapestries, Derby porcelain and 16th century Florentine bronzes and alabaster pieces.

www.muncaster.co.uk

Naworth Castle
Brampton CA8
Telephone: 01697 73229

Built by the Dacre family in 1335 and subsequently occupied by the EWarls of Carlisle, now owned by Philip Howard. Restored after 1844 fire by Webb and Burne-Jones. Contains Gobelin Tapestries, Bridal Suite, Old Library and Chapel.

www.naworth.co.uk

Rydal Mount
Ambleside LA22
Telephone: 01539 433002

Home of William Wordsworth from 1813-1850. Family portraits, personal relics and mementoes of the poet and his family.

www.rydalmount.co.uk

Sizebergh Castle
Kendal LA8
Telephone: 015395 60951

Strickland Family residence for 750 years. Contains period furniture and family portraits.

www.nationaltrust.org.uk/w-sizerghcastlegarden

Townend
Troutbeck Windemere LA23
Telephone: 01539 432628

Yeoman Farmers House from 1626, includes relics of past occupancy accumulated by the Browne family to 1943.

www.nationaltrust.org.uk/main/
w-townend

Wordsworth House
Main Street Cockermouth CA13
Telephone: 01900 820884
Birthplace of William Wordsworth in 1770. Holds mementoes of the poet, with video display

www.wordsworthhouse.org.uk

WALES
*Glamorgan, Gwent,
Gwynned, Powys*

CLWYD & DYFED

Bodelwyddan Castle
St.Asaph, Clwyd
Telephone: 01745 584060

A Victorian mansion which houses a collection on loan from The National Portrait Gallery, and treasures from the Victoria and Albert Museum.

www.bodelwyddan-castle.co.uk

Bodrhyddan Hall
Rhuddlan Clwyd LL18 5SB
Telephone: 01745 590414

Family home contains period furniture, armour and ancient antiquities.

www.bodrhyddan.co.uk

Chirk Castle
Chirk, Wrexham, Clwyd LL14
Telephone: 01691 777701

Built in 1310 the castle includes decorative interior detail, fine period furniture and fittings, with ancestral portraits.

www.nationaltrust.org.uk/main/
w-chirkcastle

Erddig
Wrexham Clwyd LL13
Telephone: 01978 355314

Period roomsets of smithy, sawmill, laundry, bakehouse. State rooms contain 18th/19th century furnishings.

www.nationaltrust.org.uk/
main/w-erddig

St.Davids Bishop' Palace
St David's SA62
Telephone: 01443 336000

The Bishops Palace of St.Davids contains many intriguing architectural ornaments, dating from early medieval times.

www.castlewales.com/sdbishop

GLAMORGAN

Cardiff Castle
Castle Street Cardiff CF1
Telephone: 01222 822083

Features the imaginative medievalist interiors of William Burges (1827-1881) created for the Third Marquess of Bute, ranging from themes of Alchemy and Astrology to fabled splendours of the Middle East.

www.castlewales.com/cardiff

Castell Coch
Tonggwynlais Cardiff CF15
Telephone: 01222 810101

Property of the Lord Bute built on site of medieval castle, and decorated with celebrated Aesops Fables.

www.wales360.co.uk/castell_coch/

Bodelwyddan Castle
Source: Wikipedia

GWENT

Blaenavon Ironworks
Nr Brecon Beacons National Park
Blaenavon
Telephone: 01495 792615

Ironworks founded in the 18th century displays original furnaces and machinery.

www.blaenavontic.com

Penhow Castle
nr Newport Gwent NP6
Telephone: 01633 400800

Ancestral home of the Seymours. Includes Norman bedchamber, and 15th century Hall and Minstrels Gallery.

www.castlewales.com/penhow

Tredegar House
Newport NP1
Telephone: 01633 815880

Morgan family residence for 500 years, redesigned in 17th century, with series of State Rooms, but retaining Medieval courtyard. Rooms decorated in period styles with recreated interiors and servants' quarters.

www. newport.gov.uk/_dc/inde/tredegarhouse

GWYNNEDD

Aberconwy House
Castle Street Conwy LL32
Telephone: 01492 592246

14th century merchants house, with period room sets and audio-visual display.

www.aboutbritain.com/AberconwyHouse

Bryn Bras Castle
Llanrug, Caernarfon LL55
Telephone: 01286 870210

Neo-classical building of 1830 contains

family collection of furniture and fittings, stained glass and decorative ornaments.

www.brynbrascastle.co.uk/castle

Penhryn Castle
Bangor LL57
Telephone: 01248 371337

Constructed in Neo-Norman style by Thomas Hopper, from 1820-45. Houses significant collection of paintings. Also an industrial railway museum.

www.nationaltrust.org.uk/main/w-penrhyncastle

Plas Newydd
Llanfairpwll, Anglesey LL61
Telephone: 01248 715272

Designed by James Wyatt , 18th century mansion overlooking the Menai Strait includes main collection of Rex Whistler's work. Also a military museum.

www. nationaltrust.org.uk/main/
w-plasnewydd

Portmeiron
Portmeiron LL48
Telephone: 01766 772311

Fantasy environment designed by Sir Clough Williams Ellis, and setting for '60s cult series The Prisoner

www.portmeirion-village.com

POWYS

Powys Castle
Weshpool Powys
Telephone: 01938 551944

Medieval fortress holds Clive Family Collection of Indian treasures.

www. nationaltrust.org.uk/powys

Trewern Hall
Trewern Welshpool SY21
Telephone: 01938 570243

Chapman family residence from 1918, house dates from 1610. Collection of period memorabilia

www.britainexpress.com/
attractions.htm?attraction=684

SCOTLAND

Highland, Grampian, Tayside, Central, Fife, Lothian, Strath-clyde, Tayside, Dumfries & Galloway, and the Borders

BORDERS

Abbotsford House
Melrose Roxburghshire TD6
Telephone: 01896 752043

The residence of author Sir Walter Scott holds armour collection, personal memerobilia and library of c.9000 volumes.

www.scottsabbotsford.co.uk

Bowhill
Selkirk TD7
Telephone: 01750 22204

Home of the Buccleuch family and memorialised by Scott in *TheLay of the Last Minstrel.* Contains works by Van Dyck, Gainsborough, Raeburn and Wilkie; Meissen and Sevres porcelain.

www.bowhill.org

Duns Castle
Duns Berwickshire TD11
Telephone: 01361 883 211

Hay Family residence since 1696, 14th century fortress includes richly embellished interiors.

www.dunscastle.co.uk

Floors Castle
Kelso Roxburghshire TD5
Telephone: 01573 223333

Imposing early 18th century building designed by William Adam for the First Duke of Roxburgh, with comprehensive collection of period furniture, Chinese porcelain and many works of art.

www.roxburghe.net

Manderston
Duns, Berwickshire TD11
Telephone: 01361 882 636

Rebuilt in 1905 Manderston includes State Rooms, period furnishings and a complete silver staircase.

www.manderston.co.uk

Mellerstain House
Gordon, Berwickshire TD3
Telephone: 01573 410225

Residence of The Earl of Haddington. Georgian mansion by William and Robert Adam houses fine paintings and furniture, with classic Adam fireplace.

www.mellerstain.com

Old Gala House
Scot Crescent Galasiels TD1
Telephone: 01896 752611

Home of the Laird of Gala, with historical display of the house. Includes 1635 painted ceiling of note.

www.galashiels.bordernet.co.uk/oldgalahouse

Paxton House
Berwick-upon-Tweed TD15
Telephone: 01289 386291

Holds Chippendale Furniture and paintings on loan from the National Galleries of Scotland.

www.paxtonhouse.co.uk

Robert Smails Printing Works
High Street, Innerleithen,
Peeblesshire EH44
Telephone: 0844 4932259

A restored Victorian printing works with the original machines in working order. Archive posters on display.

www.nts.org.uk/Property/52

Thirlestane Castle
Thirlestane, Lauder,
Berwickshire TD2
Telephone: 01578 722430

Early medieval castle holds collections of historical portraits, toys and local memorabilia. Decorated ceilings and interiors.

www.thirlestanecastle.co.uk

DUMFRIES & GALLOWAY

Broughton House
High Street Kirkcudbright DG6
Telephone: 01557 330437

Home from 1901-33 of Glasgow Boys artist, AE Hornel. Collection of the artist and his contemporaries, and private library.

www.kirkcudbright.co.uk/oldhighst/broughtn

Carlyle's Birthplace
The Arched House, Ecclefechan,
Dumfrieshire
Telephone: 0844 4932247

The birthplace of the essayist and reformer Thomas Carlyle in 1795. Small museum of personal relics: photographs and manuscripts.

www.nts.org.uk/Property/60

Drumlanrig Castle
Thornhill Dumfriesshire DG3
Telephone: 01848 331555

Built in the late 17th century for the First Duke of Queensberry, Drumlanrig is decorated in the grand manner with art in its collection by Leonardo, Holbein and Rembrandt.

www.drumlanrig.com

FIFE & CENTRAL SCOTLAND

Callendar House
Calendar Park, Falkirk FK1
Telephone: 01324 503 770

Display of period room sets which programme of temporary historical exhibitions of the house.

www.undiscoveredscotland.co.uk/callendarhouse

Hill of Tarvit Mansionhouse
Cupar Fife KY15
Telephone: 0844 493 2185

The Edwardian home of the industrialist FB Sharp. Includes his extensive collections of Chippendale furniture, porcelain, bronzes, and paintings byRaeburn, Ramsay and the Dutch School.

www.aboutbritain.com/hilloftarvitmansionhouse

Kellie Castle
Pittenweem Fife KY10
Telephone: 0844 493 2184

14th century castle with richly decorated interior and examples of period furniture.

www.rampantscotland.com/visit/blvisitkellie

GRAMPIAN

Ballindalloch Castle
Grantown-on-Spey, Banffshire AB37
Telephone: 01807 500206

Interesting collection of 17th century Spanish paintings gathered by Sir John Macpherson-Grant during the mid 19th century.

www.ballindallochcastle.co.uk

Balmoral Castle
Balmoral, Ballater, Aberdeenshire AB35
Telephone: 013397 42534

Holiday residence of the Royal Family, holds works of art exhibited in the Ballroom.

www.balmoralcastle.com

Drum Castle
Drumoak by Banchory AB31
Telephone: 0844 493 2161
The Irvine Family Estate since 13th century, castle contains extensive collection of paintings and furniture.

www.nts.org.uk/Property/24

Duff House
Banff AB45
Telephone: 01261 818181
William Adam neo-Barogue mansion built 1735. Outstation for the National Galleries of Scotland.
www.duffhouse.org.uk

Fasque
Fettercairn, Kincardineshire AB30
Telephone: 01330 850689

Home of William Gladstone, Victorian Prime Minister. Retains original interiors and settings.

www.fasque.com

Fyvie Castle
Turriff Aberdeenshire AB53
Telephone: 0844 493 2182

Includes works by Pompeo Batoni, Romney, Gainsborough and Hoppner, and collection of arms and armour.

www.nts.org.uk/Functions/Venue/11

THE HIGHLANDS

Brodie Castle
Forres Moray IV36
Telephone: 0844 493 2156

Richly embellished interior of imposing castle, with extensive art collection, and decorative objects.

www.castles.org/chatelaine/brodie

Cawdor Castle
Nairn IV12
Telephone: 01667 404401

14th century castle with 17th century additions, with family collection of portraits, tapestries, furniture and fitting.

www.cawdorcastle.com

Dunrobin Castle
Golspie, Sutherland KW10
Telephone: 01408 633177

Extensive range of period furniture, paintings and ceremonial garments in 13th century castle.

www.dunrobincastle.co.uk

LOTHIAN

Arthur Lodge
60 Dalkeith Road Edinburgh EH16
Telephone: 0131 667 5163

Neo-classical Georgian residence with Italianate sunken garden. Restored and redecorated in period manner.

www. tripwolf.com/en/guide/
show/245768/Scotland

Dalmeny House
South Queensferry Edinburgh EH30
Telephone: 0131-331 1888

Family home of the Roseberrys. Extensive holdings of Gainsborough, Reynolds. Raeburn and Lawrence. Fine 18th century French furniture.

www.dalmeny.co.uk

Edinburgh Castle
Edinburgh Lothian
Telephone: 0131 225 9846

Historic site traces Scotland's Royal heritage, with access to the Crown Room and Vaults.

www.edinburghcastle.gov.uk

Gosford House
Longniddry East Lothian EH32

Robert Adams designed main building, which includes celebrated Marble Hall. Extensive art collection.

www.gosfordhouse.co.uk

Lauriston Castle
2a Cramomnd Road South Edinburgh EH4
Telephone: 0131-336 2060

www. castleuk.net/castle_lists_scotland/lauristoncastle

National Gallery of Scotland
The Mound Edinburgh EH2
Telephone: 0131 624 6200

Includes works by El Greco, Verrochio, Raphael, Velazquez, Poussin and Rembrandt. Major drawings and print collections.

www.nationalgalleries.org

Palace of Holyroodhouse
Edinburgh EH8
Telephone: 0131 556 5100

Owned by HM the Queen, a palace of complex and remarkable history.

www. royal.gov.uk/ThePalaceofHolyroodhouse

National Museum of Scotland
Chambers Street Edinburgh EH1
Telephone: 0300 123 6789 0300

Natural History, Geology, and military history. Major holding of decorative and applied arts.

www.nms.ac.uk/our_museums/national_museum

Scottish National Gallery of Modern Art
75 Belford Road Edinburgh EH4
Telephone: 0131 624 6558

National collection of modern art including Picasso, Braque, Leger, Giacometti, to Paolozzi, Bellany and Hamilton Finlay.

www. aboutscotland.co.uk/edin/**arts**ngma

National Portrait Gallery
1 Queen Street Edinburgh
Telephone: 0131 624 6200

Lely, Reynolds, Ramsay, Lavery, Nicholson and Kokoschka, form part of the significant gathering of period to contemporary portraits.

www.nationalgalleries.org/portraitgallery

Talbot Rice Gallery
West College Street, Edinburgh EH1
Telephone: 0131 650 2210

A collection of historic photographs, complemented by changing exhibitions of contemporary artists.

www.trg.ed.ac.uk

Little Sparta
Stonypath, Dunsyre, Carnwath,
Lanarkshire ML11
Telephone: 01899 810252

The home and garden of the poet and artist Ian Hamilton Finlay (1925-2006)A place created with script and sculpture to form a haven for reflection.

www.littlesparta.co.uk

STRATHCLYDE

Bachelors Club
Sandgate Street Tarbolton KA5
Telephone: 01292 541940

Site of Robert Burns meeting place for debates in 1780. Relics and mementoes of the poet, with period room sets.

www.nts.org.uk/Property/7/

Blairqhan Castle
Straiton Maybole Ayshire KA19
Telephone: 01655 770239

Built in 1821-24 Blairqhan houses unaltered room sets with Regency fittings.
www.blairquhan.co.uk

Burns Cottage
Alloway Ayrshire KA7
Telephone: 0131 624 6426

Birthplace of renowned Scots poet now preserved as a museum.

www.robertburns.org

Burrell Collection
Pollock Country Park, 2060
Pollokshaws Road, Glasgow G3
Telephone: 0141 287 2550

Formed by Sir William and Lady Burrell, a collection of c.8000 artefacts gathered over eighty years to 1958; includes Middle Eastern, Egyptian,Greek, Chinese and Japanese art and objects.

www.thinkscotland.net/glasgow/burrell

Glasgow Art Gallery and Museum
Kelvingrove Glasgow G3
Telephone: 0141-357 3929

Natural history, geology and archeology of Scotland; arms and armour; art collection including Botticelli, Giorgione,Rembrandt, Delacroix, and Salvador Dali's celebrated painting of *St John on The Cross.*

www.glasgowlife.org.uk/museums/our-museums

Glasgow School of Art
167 Renfrew Street Glasgow G3
Telephone: 0141 276 9599

Designed by Charles Rennie Mackintosh, renowned school houses collection of the architects furniture, drawings, models and plans.

www.gsa.ac.uk

Hunterian Art Gallery
Gilbert Scott Building
University Avenue,Glasgow G12
Telephone: 0141 330 4221

Extensive collection of 20th century prints and drawings including Scottish printmakers and 20th century master such as Bomberg and Auerbach.

www.hunterian.gla.ac.uk

The Hill House
Upper Colqhoun Street
Helensburgh G84
Telephone: 0844 493 2208

Significant creation of advanced architect Charles Rennie Mackintosh, also includes his furniture and fittings.

www.nts.org.uk/Property/58

TAYSIDE

Angus Folk Museum
Kirkwynd Glamis Forfar Angus DD8
Telephone: 0844 493 2141

Six 19th century cottages house original agricultural implements, with historical displays of farming history.

www.nts.org.uk/Property/5/

Meigle Sculptured Stone Museum
Meigle Tayside
Telephone: 01828 640612

Collection of twenty five sculptured monuments from the Celtic Christian era.

www. aboutbritain.com/ MeigleSculpturedStoneMuseum

The Pier Arts Centre
Victoria Street, Stromness, Orkney
Telephone: 01856 850209

Established in 1979, the Pier holds in trust a collection of contemporay and 20th c.British art, donated by peace activist and philanthropist Margaret Gardiner (1904-2005). Changing programme of temporary and themed exhibitions.

www.pierartscentre.com

Recommended further reading with acknowledgements from Cv/Visual Arts Research:

Julian Honer (ed) *The Art Directory* (London: Macmillan)

Hudsons Historic Houses and Gardens (Banbury, Oxon: Norman Hudson & Co)

The National Trust Handbook (The National Trust Publications)

Maigle Sculptured Stone
Meigle Sculptured Stone Museum
Blairgowrie Tayside

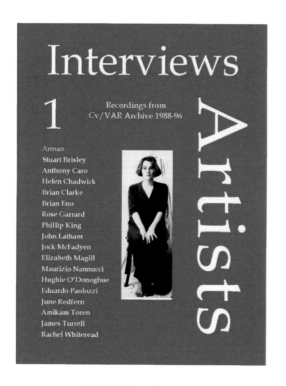

ISBN 978-1905571-50-5

ISBN 978-0956520-24-1

ISBN 978-1908419-00-2

Small

Histories

Studies of Western Art

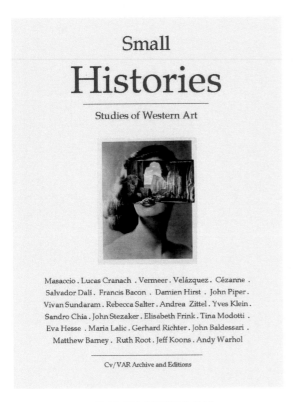

Masaccio . Lucas Cranach . Vermeer . Velázquez . Cézanne .
Salvador Dalí . Francis Bacon . Damien Hirst . John Piper .
Vivan Sundaram . Rebecca Salter . Andrea Zittel . Yves Klein .
Sandro Chia . John Stezaker . Elisabeth Frink . Tina Modotti .
Eva Hesse . Maria Lalic . Gerhard Richter . John Baldessari .
Matthew Barney . Ruth Root . Jeff Koons . Andy Warhol

Cv/VAR Archive and Editions

ISBN 978-0956520-27-2

Curators and

Collections

Volume Two:
Foundations and Initiatives

The Art Fund . Contemporary Art Society . The Ashmolean
Museum . Dulwich Picture Gallery . Arts Council Collection .
Yorkshire Sculpture Park . Independent curators and gallerists .
Private Foundations . Collections Guide:
England, Wales and Scotland.

Cv/VAR Archive and Editions

ISBN 978-0956520-21-0

Albion

Dreams of the City

N.P.James

ISBN 978-1908419-19-4

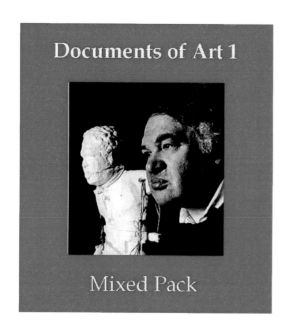

ISBN 978-1908419-04-0   ISBN 978-190841-13-2

Documents of Art 1 Recordings 1988-2010 from Cv/VAR archive. WAV audio files are re-mastered from the original tapes. Includes pdf reader of transcripts. **Features: Billy Apple** Apple Brand . **Arman** Destruction-Creation . **Morag Ballard** Stages of Invention **Anthony Caro** Steel Eye Span . **Helen Chadwick** Of Mutability . **Jim Dine** Telephone Call **Rose Garrard** Area for Conversation . **Rachel Goodyear** Wildlife Encounters . **Phillip King** Shogun . **John Latham** Story of RIO . **Jock McFadyen** Grandeur & Graffiti . **David Nash** Family Tree . **Hughie O'Donoghue** Sleeper . **Eduardo Paolozzi** Newton Figures . **Michael Porter** Close to the Ground . **Gérard Titus-Carmel** Dédicaces . **Amikam Toren** Actualities . **James Turrell** Inside-Outside . **Rachel Whiteread** Ghost . **Alison Wilding** Harbour .

9781908419040 **Documents of Art 1** GBP £19.99 (inc. Vat)
DVD bundled with two books: I-A V1 and I-A V2 £29.95 Keywords Artist Audio BIC Classif. AF

978190841132 **Documents of Art 2** DVD contains seventy monographs as pdf files £19.99

9781908411200 **Documents of Art 3** DVD contains audio files of curator interviews 1989-2011 £19.99

978190841170 **Documents of Art 4** DVD contains 400 pages as pdf files scanned from eleven issues of Cv Journal 1988-91. £19.99

Cv/VAR researchers:

Nicholas James studied painting with Keith Vaughan and Frank Auerbach at the Slade School of Art, UCL, printmaking at the Curwen Press and History of Art (MA) at Kingston University. He is the publisher and series editor of Cv Publications.

Sarah James studied fine art at Goldsmiths and Wimbledon School of Art, with further training in counselling at complementary medicine. She was co-editor of Cv Journal of Art and Crafts 1988-91 and since contributed to several titles of Cv Publications.

For catalogue information of Cv titles in print contact:
Cv Publications . 10 Barley Mow Passage .
Chiswick . London . W4 4PH UK
Tel: +44(0)20 8400 6160
www.tracksdirectory.ision.co.uk